Please
Sign In

___ ___ ___
___ ___ ___
___ ___ ___
___ ___ ___
___ ___ ___
___ ___ ___
___ ___ ___
___ ___ ___

COLLABORATIVE ART JOURNALS
AND SHARED VISIONS
IN MIXED MEDIA

COLLABORATIVE ART JOURNALS
AND SHARED VISIONS
IN MIXED MEDIA

L.K. LUDWIG

BEVERLY MASSACHUSETTS

QUARRY BOOKS

First published in the United States of America by
Quarry Books, a member of
Quayside Publishing Group
100 Cummings Center
Suite 406-L
Beverly, Massachusetts 01915-6101
Telephone: (978) 282-9590
Fax: (978) 283-2742
www.quarrybooks.com

Library of Congress Cataloging-in-Publication Data
Ludwig, L. K.
  Collaborative art journals and shared visions in mixed media / L.K. Ludwig.
    p. cm.
  Includes index.
  ISBN-13: 978-1-59253-520-0
  ISBN-10: 1-59253-520-8
  1. Photographs--Conservation and restoration. 2. Scrapbook journaling. 3. Altered books. I. Title.
  TR465.L89 2009
  745.593--dc22

2008046112
CIP

ISBN-13: 978-1-59253-520-0
ISBN-10: 1-59253-520-8

10 9 8 7 6 5 4 3 2 1

Design: Laura H. Couallier,
  Laura Herrmann Design
Photography: Lightstream

Printed in China

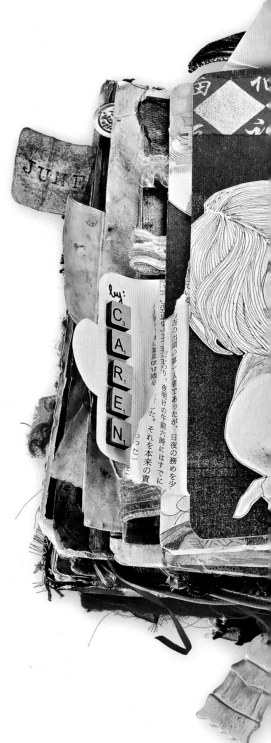

above: Work by Caren McNee; previous page by Ruth Rae

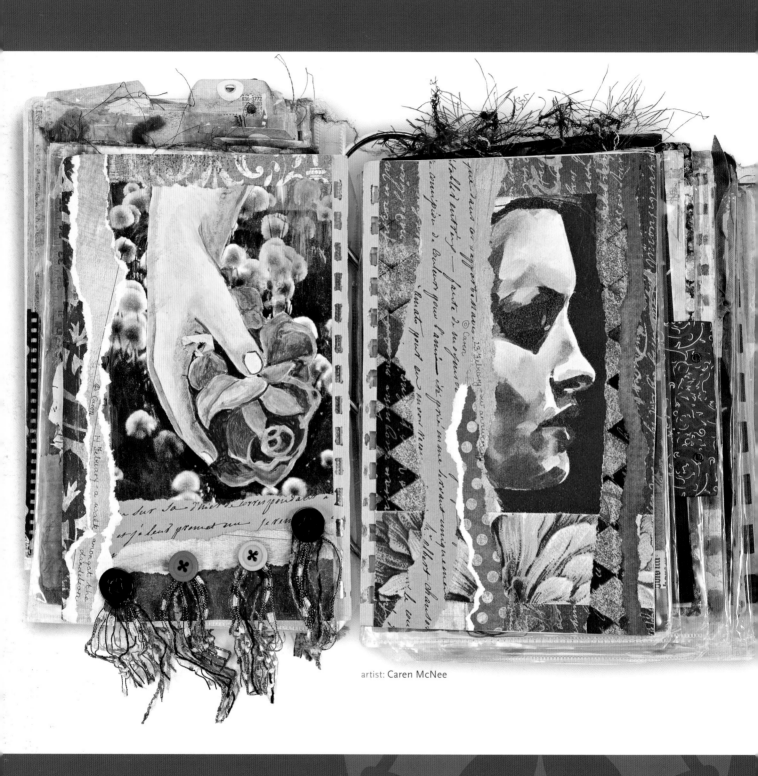

artist: Caren McNee

CONTENTS

INTRODUCTION

WORKING AS AN ARTIST IS OFTEN A VERY SOLITARY EXPERIENCE. IN STUDIOS, SPARE ROOMS, AND ON DINING ROOM TABLES, WE WORK WITHOUT THE COMPANY OF OTHER ARTISTS AS WE PAINT, DRAW, COLLAGE, AND ASSEMBLE OUR WORK IN JOURNALS, ON PAINTINGS, AND IN OUR MIXED-MEDIA PIECES.

As artists, we work into the pieces, adding, subtracting, setting aside, revisiting, discarding, and proceeding. There is a process of creating that varies for each artist, but in general, most of those moment-to-moment decisions about what to do next, and the bigger decisions of where our work is leading us, are made on our own. Some of us live where there are large communities of artists, and we can gather a collection of fellow creatives whose work resonates with us, with whom we can share work, ideas, process, and friendship. But for many of us, that community does not exist or is limited in scope. We create connections at regional and national workshops, via blogging, and by email. The Internet, once ballyhooed as something that would isolate people from each other, has had quite the opposite effect on the artistic community, offering artists new ways to connect with each other. From these connections, online artistic communities form, artist bloggers find and link to each other, and artistic dialogues begin. Friendships and collaborations bloom. Plans are made for artistic exchanges, art journals traverse the country and the globe, and we gather wherever we can, excited by the prospect of meeting other artists whom we have known only online.

The artistic collaborations explored here encompass a broad swath of art media and come in many forms—art journals, altered books, three-dimensional pieces, retreat swaps, mail art, and virtual exchanges. Some of the collaborations you will see have been ongoing for years, while others have been short, finite exchanges. What is true about all of these collaborations is that they offered the opportunity to explore a *shared vision*, to examine a topic from a variety of artistic viewpoints, to work on a common theme with one's individual artistic style, and to reach out to other artists to create a global community.

At ten years old
I pester my grandmother
to take me when she
picks up my aunt at
"the shop"—
a low slung building
up the west
where Italian women
sew cheek to cheek
until the bell rings
at 4:00 &
the electricity is cut
to create a roar
of silence.

The smell of freshly
pressed fabric
mingles with the grease
of the machines
and in my youth
I ignore the women's
hunched backs and slippered feet
and I head for barrels
where I burrow
head first into
scraps trimmed with
sequins beads lace
and gypsy colors
of satin and tulle.

I gather my scraps
for Barbie dresses
and window curtains
and pester my aunt
to make gowns from
sapphire taffetas &
ruby red silks
hand smocked sun dresses
bridal veils from tattered
mantillas
shreds of velvet a
pillbox hat.

40 years later
we divvy up the
off-the-shoulder ballgowns &
argue over the provenance of the
hand-beaded wedding dress
and the smell of
fresh ironing
is a heady narcotic
for my soul.

So I began my life
as a bagpicker,
magpie hunter of shiny things
always diving head first into
piles of junk
in order to grab
the gypsy things.

THE ARTISTIC CONVERSATION

IT CERTAINLY DIDN'T BEGIN WITH PICASSO AND MATISSE, BUT
IN 2003, MoMA'S EXHIBIT THAT EXAMINED THEIR LIFELONG
DIALOGUE SPOTLIGHTED THE IDEA THAT TWO ARTISTS, VERY
DIFFERENT IN STYLE AND PERSONALITY, COULD FORGE A RELA-
TIONSHIP THAT SPANNED DECADES AND SPURRED BOTH OF THEM
FORWARD TO GREATER GENIUS.

John Berger and John Christie collaborated and in 2000 produced the beguiling book, *I Send You This Cadmium Red,*
in which they showcased their correspondence in words,
color, and line.

The artistic conversation arises naturally when artists
connect. When those artists are separated by distance,
those conversations begin to flow through the Internet and
the mail. Many times, artists meet through the Internet.
A comment posted on a blog sparks a conversation, or an
exchange in an email community launches a private email dialogue,
and the seeds of a friendship are sown. Discussions of family life, relationships,
and hopes occur, personal histories are gradually revealed, the ups and downs
of the artistic life are shared, and art is part of this process. Many times art is
exchanged as gifts, and frequently an artistic conversation begins through a
collaborative process—art journals, altered books, or sketchbooks travel back and
forth between friends, saying as much in art as is said in words. This process is
both comforting and risky. Worries arise—will the work be well received? Will it
be disappointing? Will it say too much? Or not enough? But it is this risk that can
grow an artistic friendship into the kind of relationship that spans years and
distance, divorces and moves, joys and sorrows.

1

Loretta Marvel and Dana Jenkins correspond in this
watercolor journal called TRANS4M8TIONS.

A FACE-TO-FACE
Artistic Conversation

Tara Ross and Katie Kendrick decided to exchange journals. Both women have unique artistic styles, but having seen the two artists' work together, it is easy to see why they were drawn (pun intended) to each other's work. The following Inner-view with Katie discusses some aspects of their artistic conversation:

below: Journal entry by Katie Kendrick in Tara Ross' journal

"It has been said that art is a tryst,
for in the joy of it, maker and beholder meet."
—Kojiro Tomita

INNER-VIEW WITH ARTIST KATIE KENDRICK

What prompted the two of you to exchange journals? How did the conversation begin?

I got an email from Tara, asking if I'd be interested in doing a journal exchange so that we could do some artwork in one another's books. I jumped on it as I'm a big fan of Tara's artwork, and loved the idea of having some of it parked in my big old book.

The topic/theme/starting point seems to be faces. How did that come to be? Tell me about what the topic meant to you personally.

I remember Tara asking me if I had a topic or theme that I wanted her to use when she worked in my book. I told her that I would like her to feel free to do whatever she felt like in my book, that I wanted her to work spontaneously and freely, like she does in her personal work. When I asked her that same question, she responded the same way—she wanted me to just work intuitively and from the heart. Because conveying emotions, thoughts, and events through faces and simple figures seems to be central to the artwork that both Tara and I create, I don't think either one of us was surprised to see that it was a thread we both chose to carry out in all our pieces for one another.

Did you know each other well prior to beginning? Had you ever met in person? Was there anything gained in your relationship as part of the exchange process?

We met one another online a couple years before the journal exchange. I can remember the first time I saw Tara's work—I loved the edgy outsider quality it had, and some of the pieces, although simple, touched me deeply. I don't remember who exactly introduced themselves to the other first—I think I initially left a comment on Tara's blog. And that's how our relationship began—we would visit one another's blogs, where we both would post our latest artwork, and comment. That grew into occasional emails and then we finally met one another at ArtFest (a national art workshop held annually), where we had made arrangements to meet up and trade original paintings with one another. So although we both already had paintings on canvas made by one another, there was a certain intimacy and sense of honor that came with working in each other's personal journal, something more private somehow, and I clearly experienced a stronger connection with both Tara and her art after the exchange.

top: Katie Kendrick's work in Tara Ross's journal

left: A journal page spread done by Tara Ross in Katie Kendrick's journal

FAMILY MATTERS
Collaborating at Home

As artists, sometimes we find our strongest way of sharing, of communicating our feelings, is done visually. In a family where there is more than one artist, interesting visual conversations can occur. Often family collaborations occur with a parent and child. The time spent making art together gives the parent and child quality time, and the activity enriches the children's creativity and problem-solving skills. Art techniques are taught through the natural course of the process. We long to share the experience and pleasure of creating with our offspring, and we have spent countless hours "enriching" their experiences with paint, crayons, pencils, and clay. It is no surprise that they feel perfectly at liberty to add to one of our works that might be out on the worktable. It was just this type of scenario that resulted in the collaborative puppet L.K Ludwig made with her six-year-old daughter, Maggie.

above: *Urban Crow* was created by L.K. and Maggie Ludwig.

When my daughter was about seven years old, she asked me one day what I did at work. I told her I worked at the college—that my job was to teach people how to draw. She stared at me, incredulous, and said, "You mean they forget?"

—HOWARD IKEMOTO

She had just begun a series of puppets with bodies that were essentially paintings on canvas. She had left the puppet body for the blackbird piece on the table and while she was away, her daughter drew a skyline on some paper. She presented it to her mother as the place where the crow flies among the tall empty buildings like a canyon. Using a white gel marker, she drew in her canyon of abandoned high-rises. The gel marker allowed them to wipe clean any smudges or marks Maggie didn't want. They sealed it with clear matte sealer once the ink was dry.

This mixed-media painting on wood (above) by Carla Sonheim and her son Wes occurred spontaneously. Carla was starting a new painting, and Wes, who was eleven, literally grabbed the charcoal from her hand and started drawing. Carla had blocked out the girl and a cow, but Wes added in the cow's eyes and expression, as well as the sun, moon, mountains, and the ground lines. Carla said, "At first I almost said "No!", but then I just let him at it—and it's a thousand times better because of Wes' hand. It's good not to take yourself too seriously. We have small masters all around us in the form of children."

Elizabeth Bunsen and her son Boone work together regularly in her studio in Vermont. This small green painting was done to process a difficult experience. The neighbor's puppy was injured and became paralyzed. They worked together on the piece below, creating the printing blocks for the central images and adding a hopeful thought at the bottom.

INNER-VIEW WITH
ELIZABETH BUNSEN

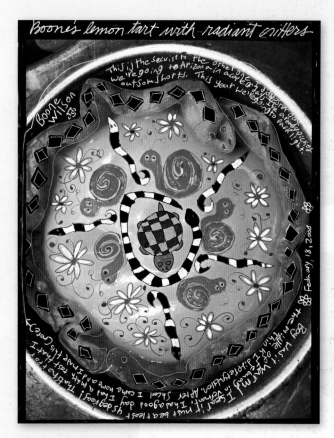

Tell me about working with Boone on a project —what is it like for you to watch him work?

Working with Boone is intense—he cares deeply, but being an artist is like breathing to him—no big deal. Boone has always had his own spin on things. When he was about three, he did a series of playground drawings that I re-created on a very large format using my nondominant hand—I sold the entire show—fourteen paintings—so we have been collaborating since he could hold a brush or pencil.

I am guessing you wedge in bits of technique teaching into the whole process. Does he direct what he is learning or do you pick something to teach?

I do wedge in suggestions—now, however, he prefers for me to suggest only when asked. With the Luna painting, Boone was very involved with the "transition" colors ... The title was my contribution; he asked me to write it, as his writing is a little funky.

I will often suggest something I know he will enjoy and then let him run with it—like Luna. We usually paint in my town studio (sometimes at home on the deck)—it is big and we can get messy.

Sometimes—rather often, actually—I consider the collaborative process as a form of visual conversation. Does working with Boone feel like that? Besides the talking about "how-to" and "where," does the conversation while working feel like more is being revealed?

Something else is being revealed ... oh yes—it is like a dance we do together. I have an MFA in painting and art history, ten years in art schools, and he is by far my greatest teacher. Boone has taught me mainly about loosening up and listening to and being guided by my intuition; he has taught me about the rapture of rawness. This is by no means a direct thing, but certainly the undercurrent for me. Oh, and Boone has to choose the music—almost always jazz, Miles Davis in particular—and he always manages to completely cover himself in paint.

above: Sisters Loretta Marvel and Maria Fazio participated in a fabric art journal collaborative with a moon theme. Loretta's art journal, *Drinking Down the Moon*, shows their work.

When two creatives are a couple, one would think that artistic collaboration flows naturally. However, this isn't always the case. Art making is often a solitary process, so conscious effort is required just like in any collaboration. The difference is that the conversation can express more because the intended viewer, the other partner, more deeply understands the content.

between

here we are in the land of closed bedroom doors, worrying about appearance, having feeling for girls who haven't noticed, wanting to be good enough, to have friends to fit in. We have reached the 'between' and I work to fill my new role as my son changes

above, opposite, and below: These journal pages by L.K. and Joe Ludwig, visually discuss their daily experiences, longings, and thoughts, along with the chance to share some beauty.

THE POWER OF
Collaborative Art

"I have made lots of friends from doing collaborative art ... a lot of my art-world friendships began with an art swap. Living in rural Tennessee, I have found the introduction of the Internet, Google, blogs, and swaps has really enlarged my world."

– Anne Bagby

"Collaborative projects change my internal perspective. I try new techniques and new materials. I often pour myself into the art for these projects in a way that I wouldn't if I were making it just for me.

– Suzanne Cook

"Most important, the collaboration process gives me license to think of myself as an artist without feeling like a pretender. Someone assumes I will create something they want to see, hold, and keep. That unspoken faith in me reassures me as I work, and helps keep the chittering negative thoughts to a minimum."

– Lisa Myers Bulmash

"Collaborative projects have taken my artwork into unexplored areas due to a particular goal or prompt that one finds in collaboration. These guidelines narrow down the choices, but broaden the artistic possibilities tremendously. I also like that these projects can span months, if not years. Working together on something through a long period of time helps connect the participants."

– Laurie Mika

"If it were not for the numerous art communities found on the Internet, I probably wouldn't call myself an artist. In my groups, I look for the common ground that I share with people who are probably very unlike me in their daily life, and I try to remain open to what I can learn from them."

– Cindy Ericsson

"As a new artist, I appreciate how I have to stretch while having the safety of the boundaries of a collaboration. I've been able to observe my own process and learn from it. I didn't even know I had a process until I had to work to a deadline. Collaborative projects are like warm-up exercises; suddenly the ideas just come flooding in."

– Tina Abbott

"One of the best things I take away from collaborative projects is the other artists' take on the theme. They give a little insight into who they are and how they think—just enough that you're left wanting to know more about that person."

– Michelle Unger

"The group process connects me to other artists, their ideas and their work, in a sustained and thoughtful way. Interacting personally with artists in a social setting is terrific—they're funny and open and bright. But the opportunity to 'talk' with them at the speed of writing or art is a unique one that gets into depth about the idea and the work (whatever that is)."

– Shirley Ende-Saxe

"I've been challenged not only by deadlines, but also by themes or subjects I may not normally work with, or even colors I don't usually work with. My creativity is stretched. I've often found that some of my personal favorite work was done in an altered book of someone else!"

– Angie Platten

"I was in a deep funk, not doing art and not caring, but I saw an article in Somerset Studio that mentioned Yahoo groups. I checked into it, and now, I have a functioning art room. It wasn't that easy, but it happened. For the first time in a long time I started referring to myself as an artist and not a wife, or mother, or clerk. And, I was making Art!"

– Joannie Hoffman

artist: Catherine Anderson, DJ Pettit

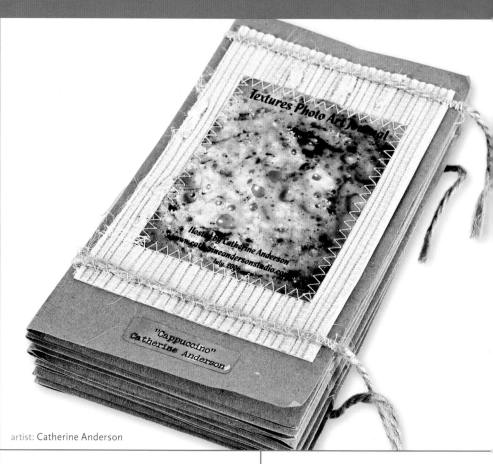

artist: Catherine Anderson

artist: Bee Shay, Gwen Delmore

artist: Bee Shay, Michele Unger

artist: Joanne Thieme Huffman, Tina Isperdulli

artist: Heather Muenstermann, Cathy Keith

PRACTICAL CONSIDERATIONS

Organizing and coordinating a collaborative project comes with its share of responsibility. There are a large number of practical considerations regarding the structure and guidelines.

While not fully comprehensive, the information that follows should help in thinking through the process of creating a swap or round robin. Take your time when creating the guidelines, then have someone else look for missing information. Provide information on your theme or topic and any rules about the topic and its ability to be stretched. Artists love to stretch boundaries.

2

left: Artwork in this collaborative journal is by Kathy Wasilewski.

DECIDING ON
a Collaborative Structure

For any given collaboration, there are many possible structures. But in general, most collaborations are either round robins, direct collaborations, or swaps/exchanges. In a round robin structure, there are a set number of participants. Each participant sends out a book or other item to be worked in or on. This book or item then travels to each participant—in a predetermined, circular order—who then adds their artistic contribution to the item. In this way, a finished collaborative piece is created by the time the item makes its way back to the originator. A direct collaboration is when two or more artists work together to create one or more objects. In a swap or exchange, artwork is exchanged for other artwork. Swaps/exchanges may be for single pieces of art in a 1:1 exchange, or each artist contributes a set number of pieces and receives a set number in return. Often the number returned is one less than what is sent, because the swap host often receives one of each artists' work as remuneration for the work involved in hosting.

below: Kari Ramstrom designed the *Wonderland* book for her submission.

Selection & Communication

You need to decide how to choose participants. Will the project be open to all members of a group? Will it be invitation only? Will you advertise for participants on blogs or listservs? Will you jury the work for acceptance? No matter how you decide to handle your selection process, be sure to include rules and expectations for participation up front, so that each potential participant is aware of the level of commitment involved. You also need to decide how communication within the group will be handled. Will members communicate by email, listserv, Yahoo group, blog, or some combination? Deciding on the type and frequency of communication will help your group meet your expectations. You should decide in advance whether you want your group to grow socially and permit everyday chatter or whether your members are interconnected sufficiently that swap-only business will be permitted. Typically, it is helpful if all participants are required to post when a piece is shipped or received.

The organizer should obtain full names, addresses, and phone numbers of all participants. Participants needn't receive phone numbers, but the correct, complete addresses for mailing are essential. The organizer also assembles the mailing order and any accompanying details, such as a chart of topics or techniques, and who will be expected to do what, where, and when. Determine how delays will be managed, and how consistently late participants will be handled. Decide whether color copies are acceptable or whether only original works can be submitted.

The structure you set up in organizing your project can help avoid disappointments. Something that organizers and participants alike should be aware of is the small risk that someone will drop out of sight and take the work he or she has into oblivion.

Another major decision is how related costs will be handled by the group. In swaps and or exchanges, participants usually pay for the costs of shipping and packaging the swap. In round-robin style collaborations that travel overseas, either the group shares the additional burden, reimbursing the members with the extra shipping costs, or some members volunteer to ship overseas.

Some other questions that need to be answered are what shipping companies will participants use, and whether items should be shipped with insurance and tracking information. Many collaborative project veterans believe that it is also important to discuss how items should be packaged. Be sure to indicate if the original packaging should be retained, and if and how it should be replaced, if necessary, due to the wear and tear of shipping.

above: Melissa McCobb Hubbell's work is shown inside Cassandra Walter's submission.

below: Art journal pages by Julie Collings

SHARING & DISTRIBUTING ARTWORK

One of the most enjoyable parts of a collaborative project can be the packaging for the final distribution of art. Included in this book, you will find instructions for making a paper bag book (see page 59). These work well to house smaller works, such as postcards or artists' trading cards (ATCs). But there are many clever ways to return a swap. Marilyn Huskamp's inchie swap returns gives you an idea of the potential (see page 102). Accordion-folded and other types of folded books, such as pocket page books and labyrinth books (also called puzzle or maze books), can showcase a swap very nicely.

above: A bouquet of inchies provides clever and cheerful packaging.

above: This fatbook page by Carol Parks is a paper bag which holds vintage ephemera.

left: This box is based on a Gothic window.

FOLDED LABYRINTH BOOKS

Made by simply folding a large sheet of paper into fourths horizontally and vertically and then some clever cutting, these books are wonderful for housing exchanges of flat, one-sided artworks. Credit lines can be applied to the reverse side or below each artwork. The reverse could also be used to hold more work.

1. You will need to lay out the work to assess what size paper you will need. Using a sufficiently large piece of paper to accommodate your project, fold into fourths horizontally and then vertically.

2. Unfold the sheet, and then cut according to the diagram. Starting with one free end, refold each segment accordion-style to create the book. Adhere artwork as desired.

KEY:

BLUE LINE = FOLD

RED LINE = CUT

3. This is an alternative cut-and-fold pattern. As above, start at one end and refold, accordion-style.

The book or journals used for collaboratives can be created in clever ways to allow participating artists room to work in varying thicknesses and media. If you step away from the idea of circulating a bound book, you permit the other participants the opportunity to work in a way that they shine, and your returned project will be the very best it can be. This is most easily done by creating a way to send along a portfolio or an unbound package of pages.

The self-portrait collaborative that was organized by Teesha Moore took nearly three years to finish and passed through twenty-six artists' hands. The variety in those structures, which ranged from boxes to bags to fabric journals to regular journals to old phonograph albums, was a testament to ingenuity. Another option is to use portfolio structures. You might consider a vintage bill-paying binder filled with the original envelopes to serve as a portfolio. Here are some other options:

below: This book cover portfolio was created using a Victorian-era photo album, a cigar box, and hand-dyed papers.

BOOK COVER PORTFOLIO BOX

Using a set of book covers with an intact spine, and an appropriately sized box, this portfolio box is simple to make and ready to embellish.

1. You will need glue, a book cover with an intact spine and pages removed, and a box with or without a lid.

2. Decorate or cover the box before proceeding.

3. Cover the inside of the spine with decorative fabric.

4. Glue the bottom of the box to the inside of your back cover.

If your covers do not have an intact spine, you can use fabric to re-create a spine. Simply cut a strip and adhere to the outside of the covers, and reinforce by adhering a strip to the inside as suggested in step 3.

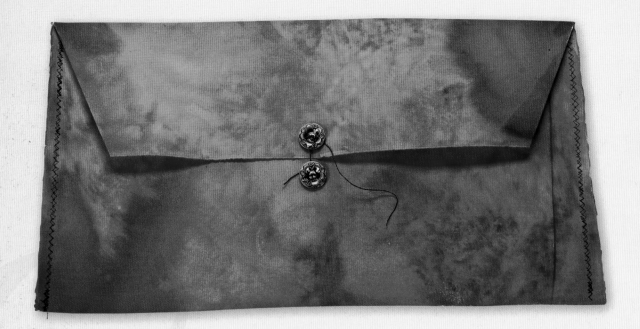

SEWN PAPER PORTFOLIO

Depending on how you choose to decorate your pocket, you can decorate before or after completion.

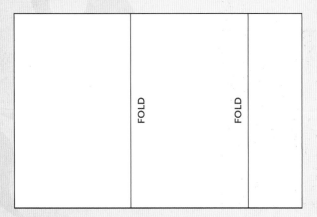

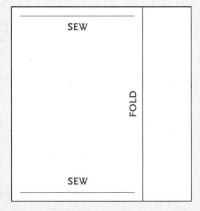

1. Using a large piece of heavy watercolor or printmaking paper; fold as if to create an envelope. You would fold it into thirds, but not equal thirds.

2. Then simply sew the sides of the larger fold to form a pocket, leaving a top flap. While glue will work, the zigzag stitch on a sewing machine works great also.

KEY:

BLUE LINE = FOLD

GREEN LINE = SEW

Some examples of simple, commercially available journals and albums ready for your embellishment are shown here. A good-quality photo album, with its heavy paper and its expandable design, makes an ideal book for a collaborative. It can be used without the plastic pockets for journaling projects, or with the plastic pockets for postcards, ATCs, or smaller paper projects. Vintage or new scrapbooks also function nicely because the pages can be removed for working on, and the screw posts can be replaced with longer ones if you want to accommodate more work. A vintage cookbook or gardening binder can be painted or covered with paper to provide an easy-to-use expandable container. A heavy folder envelope can be purchased at an office supply store and embellished.

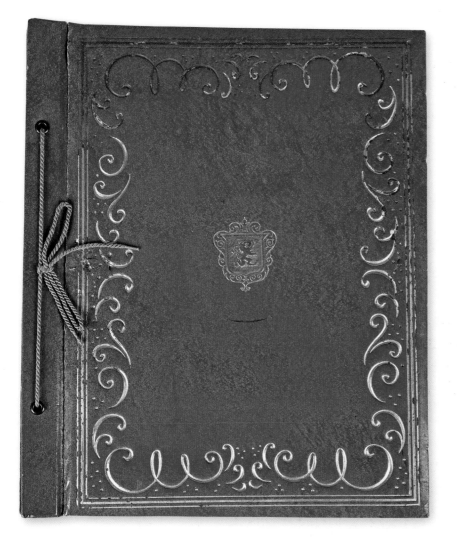

above and left: Both vintage and new scrapbooks and albums make great structures for collaborative work.

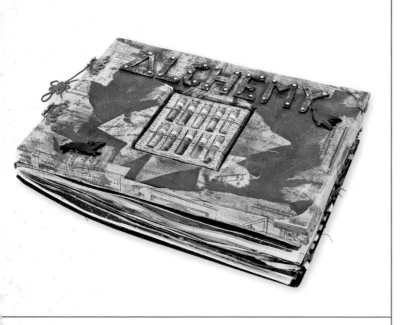

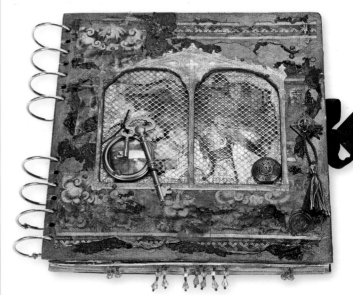

ART JOURNAL COLLABORATIVES

AN ART JOURNAL COLLABORATIVE PROJECT IS A ROUND ROBIN WHERE EACH ARTIST SENDS A BOOK OFF TO THE OTHER ARTISTS IN THE GROUP SO THAT EACH ARTIST IN TURN WORKS IN EACH BOOK, UNTIL THE PROJECT IS COMPLETE.

Variations of this structure abound, and some collaborations are done more like exchanges, with each participant producing sufficient book pages to provide a page for each group member's book. Some projects are built around artistic building blocks: color, line, style, or medium. Art journal collaborations can also be structured so that learning occurs, for example, where each artist or each round requires a different technique to be demonstrated in the work. Another kind of collaborative is done around a topic. The topic can change for each round, or the project can have one overarching theme around which each artist might work. The themes one can choose are as varied as snowflakes.

In this chapter, several examples of art journal collaboratives are shown. The *Color Play* project focused on both color and techniques. The Photo Art Journal group worked with both a specific medium and a regular theme to produce numerous books. *The Circles Art Journal* was done around a type of line, while both the *Spring Secrets* and the *Alphabet Soup* collaborations focused on a topic. A paper bag book provides a specific structure for one group while a theme is evident throughout their work.

opposite: Book covers created for the *Color Play* art journal collaborative. Clockwise from top left: Artists Lynne Porter, Lou McCulloch, Sally Turlington, and Kim Logan

"COLOR PLAY"
Art Journal Round Robin

COLOR PLAY WAS A ROUND ROBIN THAT WAS ORGANIZED BY SUE BERRY AND WAS A swap that traveled to and from the United Kingdom and across the United States. Each of the eleven participants originated one book as well as worked in each others' books. For each book, participants were assigned a technique—working with transfers, molding paste, wax collage, peeling paint, paint textures, crackled surfaces, peeling paper, working with transparencies, and wax rubbings. In addition, each technique was associated with a specific set of colors. The artists rotated through the books, working a different assigned technique and color set with the arrival of each book. This allowed the participating artists to use all of the various techniques and color sets, and the books' originators received a variety of one-of-a-kind work.

opposite: This title page was created by Kathy Wasilewski for her journal.

top: This sign-in page was created by Sue Berry.

left: Liz Smith created this quilted fabric wrap for her journal.

An email listserv was created using Yahoo groups, and a database held helpful information such as who was doing what technique and a master list of mailing addresses. In addition, the Yahoo group format allowed conversations regarding the process, mailing dates, difficulties with execution or artistic block, and lots of oohing and aaahing when the books arrived at their destinations each month.

Many of the books were sent out, along with any preferences for content, with a place for individual artists to leave their mark. Pages where the artists could sign in were created using a variety of formats such as tags, envelopes, pockets, and inchies, which also provided an artistic table of contents that offered who, what, where, and when.

above: Kathy Wasilewski created this sign-in page.

opposite/top: Artwork by Sue Berry

opposite/bottom: Artwork by Lou McCulloch

There is this cave in the air behind my body

that nobody is going to touch:

a cloister, a silence closing around a blossom of fire.

When I stand upright in the wind,

my bones turn to dark emeralds.

FLY

I am no bird,

and no net ensnares me:

SPIRIT HOUSE

I am a free human being

with an independent will.

Remember

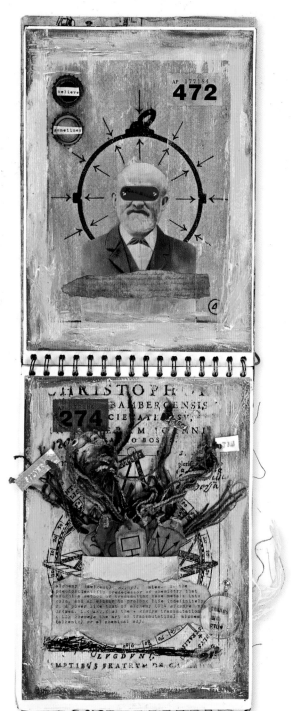

"One piece of log creates a small fire, adequate to warm you up, add just a few more pieces to blast an immense bonfire, large enough to warm up your entire circle of friends; needless to say, individuality counts, but teamwork dynamites."

—JIN KWON

above: Sue Berry

left: Sally Turlington

THE PHOTO ART
Journal Collaborative

THE PHOTO ART JOURNAL COLLABORATIVE IS A GROUP COORDINATED BY CATHERINE Anderson, a professional photographer and artist. Each book is hand assembled by Catherine in her North Carolina studio and mailed out to participants. Over-whelmingly, group members have cited Catherine's guidance and commitment to detail as what makes this group so special. Group member Vivian Montre says, "This brings me to the gratefulness I feel for being a part of this group. Catherine has held us together for a long time and her efforts make my art world a very happy place to be. Each page of the photo books represents so much thought as to color, composition, and heartfelt feelings. I really love them. The covers are wonderful. I honestly don't know which one appeals to me the most but I do know how much time it takes to create these little beauties. In this busy and cluttered world, our little books are quiet and restful."

"I always photographed what the moment told me."

—ANDRÉ KERTÉSZ

left & opposite: Work by artist
Catherine Anderson

Vancouver Downtown Eastside
a place forgotten by God
even Starbucks has no presence there!
15,000 drug injections per day
open drug peddling and shooting
$4 per doze of crystal meth makes
it quite affordable for kids and
so much quicker to forget what life
could be...

This woman in the picture lives here
who are her neighbors with blinded
windows? what are her dreams – does
she have any? does she remember
face painting fun from 30 years ago?
her empty face could have a face of
my daughter. Marushka. Is there anyone
who hugs her goodnight (free of charge)?

and how to make all those people
disappear prior to the 2010 Winter
Olympics fun so our international guests
can enjoy their lattes visually undisturbed?

by Iwona R (who saw but did nothing)

INNER-VIEW WITH
CATHERINE ANDERSON

Is there a guiding philosophy for the Photo Art Journal group?

I have been able to indulge myself in creating a group that combines many things that I love: photography, book forms, and quotations. The idea behind the group is sharing and inspiring. By sharing our photographs, we share a part of ourselves with others. We are also made to look critically at the photographs we take and understand which of them speak most soulfully to us. Some people communicate more easily in words, others in images. I prefer to communicate in image. It is easy to snap photos and leave them on your computer or in a box, but there is something healing by really taking the time to look at them and then to share that "image thought" with others. That is one of the reasons why I ask that everyone include a quotation, a poem, or their own writing on the back of the photos. By having to search for something that speaks to the photograph, they are taken deeper in to the image and really have to absorb what it is saying to them.

How long has the group existed? How often are the books produced? How are themes chosen?

The group started in 2006. We created our first book in April 2006, and since then have created books every four to six weeks. Generally, I choose the themes, but I welcome suggestions from participants and have a database open where they can include themes that appeal to them. I generally get ideas for themes from books I am reading or photographs I see.

Do you do all the bindings?

Yes, my favorite part of the process is thinking of new ways to bind the books together. During the first year most of the books were spiral bound, but then I got a little bored with doing them the same way so I started thinking of bindings that fit in with the theme. My first try at something different was the book on textures where I used an accordion book format on thick kraft paper and sewed the photos on with string to create more texture. Then I made burlap bags with the word *touch* stamped on a piece of leather and a feather on the outside of the bag. I was so excited sending these out to participants and the response was so rewarding that I carried on thinking of new ways to bind the books. One of the recent books was *Shades of White* and I made plaster pages for the back and front covers.

Samples from the Photo Art Journal
Collaborative

artist: Catherine Anderson

SHADES OF BLACK

artist: Joanne Thieme Huffman

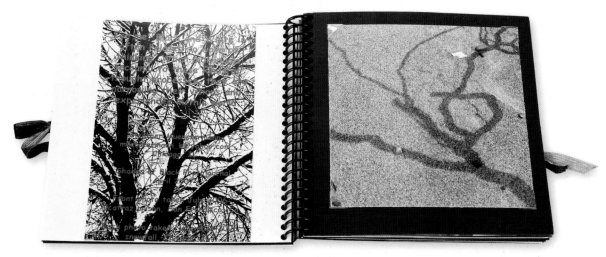

artist: Michele Unger

artist: Margot Hanson

artist: Dawn M. Shepherd

artist: Catherine Anderson

Tell me about how the Photo Art Journal group formed, and the group's system of contact and level of community. Have many of you met?

The group is operated through a Yahoo group. Group postings are mostly related to what we are doing in the group. I participated in many fat books and loved them, but my first love has always been photography, and one day it dawned on me that perhaps I could use the fat book concept to share photography. I shared this idea with Bee Shay, who encouraged me and shared the group with a number of her friends who were interested in photography. They joined up, some of my friends joined up, and we had our first book. However, one of the highlights for me was attending ArtFest in Port Townsend in 2007 and meeting a number of the group members for the first time. It was wonderful getting to meet women that I only knew through their photographs. Gwen Delmore said this about the group in one of her emails to me, "... We cherish each and every book ... there is a magic created when all of our images come together."

When working predominantly with photographs, how do you resolve the art journal versus scrapbook debate?

I think one of the ways in which these particular photo art journals are different from scrapbooks is that they collect together the various ways in which the participants interpret the world around them. Our photographs say: "This is how I see the world." And by seeing how differently we all interpret the world around us we are able to get to understand one another better and therefore connect more deeply to others. I see a scrapbook as one person's view of the world. But connecting with your own inner vision results in an image that tells a deeper story. Jan Phillips has said, "The photographs we make can be food for the soul, nourishing sustenance for the arduous and confusing journey we're on. We are all hungry for meaning, all on a quest to realize our worth, actualize our potential, manifest whatever is unique to us." This implies that every photograph we take consciously has meaning, whether it is in a photo art journal or a scrapbook. In these journals you will often find that the type of photograph is not one you would find in a scrapbook. These books are more about the world around us and the world within us than the people in our lives.

artist: Michele Unger

artist: Catherine Anderson

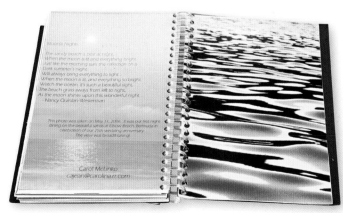

artist: Meg Sturt

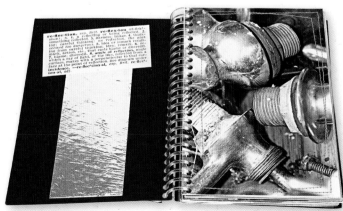

artist: DJ Pettit

SPRING SECRETS
Collaborative Project

The *Spring Secrets* collaborative project started with a blog post. Organizing artist Julie Collings read a post on Melissa McCobb Hubbell's Garden of Pink Shadows blog where Melissa described a "hankering" for a collaborative project, but one organized by someone else. Perusing the comments on the blog post, Julie spied one comment by Cassondra Walters indicating her desire to also participate in a new collaborative project and the round robin was born. The participants include Julie Collings, Melissa McCobb Hubbell, Lilia Meredith, Kari Ramstrom, and Cassondra Walters. The theme, *Spring Secrets*, came from Julie Collings: "I was right in the middle of winter and looking so forward to the spring! I wanted a theme that would stay fresh as we worked through the books. I planned to have all the books completed and back to their owners before summer. We exchanged books every two weeks."

Work from Lilia Meredith's *Spring Secrets* collaborative piece, *Sing at the Party*. The finished work fit snugly inside its hinged box. Work created by Lilia Meredith, Julie Collings, and Kari Ramstrom.

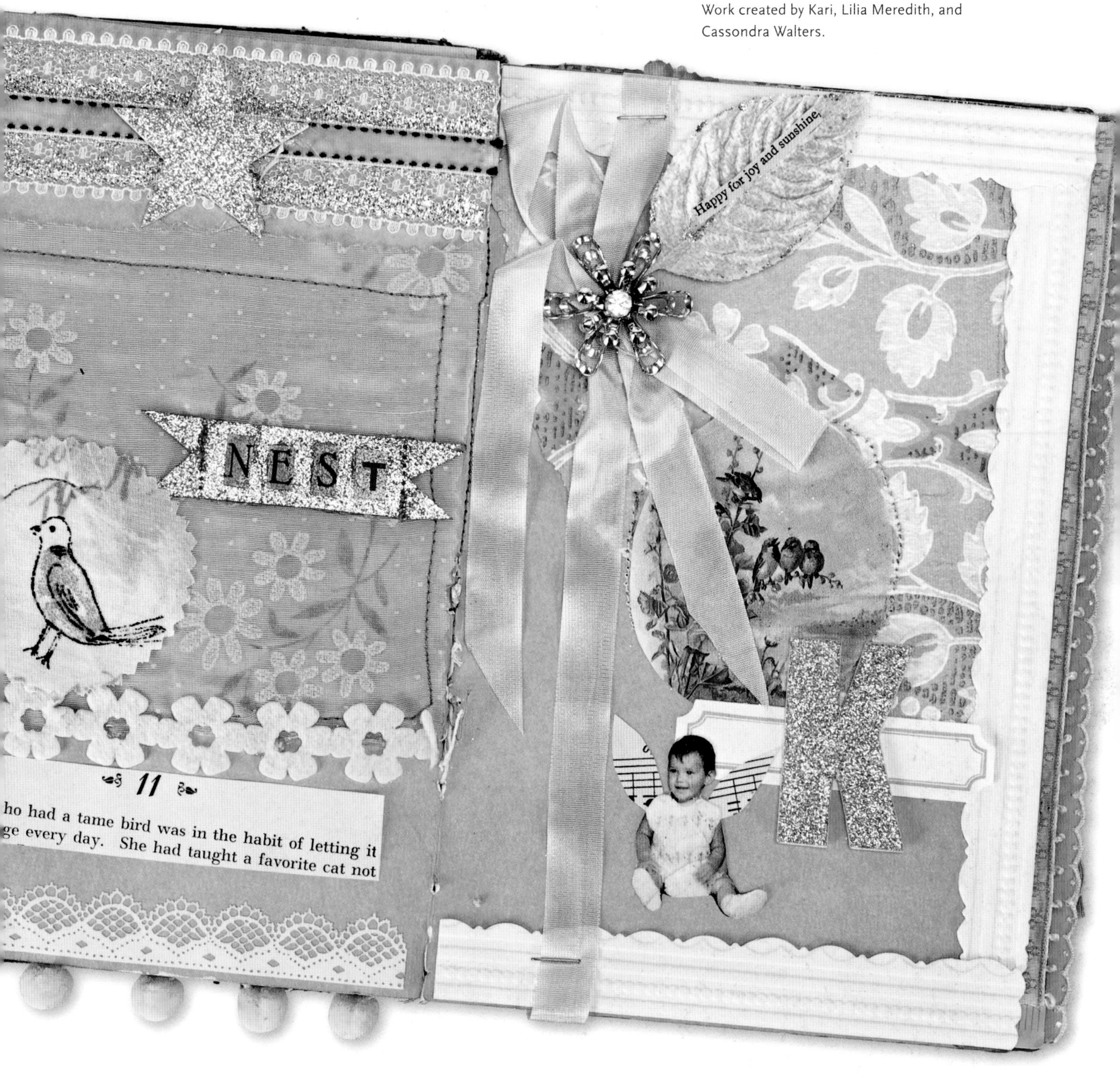
Happy for joy and sunshine.
NEST
11
ho had a tame bird was in the habit of letting it
ge every day. She had taught a favorite cat not
K

[all] Work from Kari Ramstrom's *Spring Secrets* collaborative piece, *Wonderland*. Work created by Kari, Lilia Meredith, and Cassondra Walters.

"We have technology, finally, that for the first time in human history allows people to maintain really rich connections with much larger numbers of people."

—Pierre Omidyar

SIGN IN

SPRING
ROUND
ROBIN

she listens for it.

both: Using a unique format, Cassondra Walters created her piece in a boxed set of book-shaped boxes. The participants each had a small book-shaped box in which to house their work. Work created by Cassondra Walters, Kari Ramstrom, Lilia Meredith, and Julie Collings.

An email listserv through Yahoo groups was used to organize the collaborative project and provide a forum for messages. Kari said, "Julie Collings started a Yahoo group, where we sent emails back and forth. We had some fun conversations. We all knew each other online going into the swap, but it was fun to bring us together as a group. We even had a little "spring inspiration" swap before the round robin began." These little inspiration packages were gorgeous, spring-colored packages of eye candy goodness. Many of the inclusions found their way onto the pages generated in this project. Often the packages holding the artwork had goodies enclosed for the participants. As Julie said, "I am such a sucker for packages in the mail. It was so fun to slip a little something in the box I was mailing."

Choosing the format and materials to work inside the books was something that added excitement to the process. Some items were yard sale or antique shop finds, and some were purchased with the *Spring Secrets* exchange in mind. And of course, many came from the treasured collections of the working artists.

The arrival of the packages was much anticipated by all the participants; this seems to be true across the board for all the collaborative projects. Julie, and her family, loved the arrival of the next book. She would open the box with everyone gathered around. Lilia commented that it was "like having an idea book in your hands every month!" And, as Kari said, "It's inspiring to see how others work 'in the flesh.' It is certainly different than just viewing pictures online, no matter how gorgeous the photography is. There is something about being able to handle the art, touch it, and open up all the little hidden secrets."

Sometimes after opening the artwork and examining all the work that has come before its arrival in your hands, a feeling of intimidation or doubt can surface. Working through this process in collaborative projects can help you feel more confident about your work. Julie wrote, "Participating in this project with a group of dear friends helped me to grow as an artist. It can be hard to work on another artist's pages and feel like the art is good enough. I finally stopped editing myself, and just created what I was feeling and then felt wonderful about the work I created."

All the participants also had blogs, and the participants enjoyed reading each other's posts about their daily lives and the swap, while following each other's artwork. Each has gotten a chance to meet a couple of participants at various art retreat events.

[below] Artist Julie Collings used a vintage Italian box to hold her collaborative offering, a small collection of singly bound pages.

CIRCLES
Art Journal

In this collaborative art journal, a very basic artistic element—line—is turned into an exploration of shape. Darlene Wilkinson, Gail Pierce, and Valerie Foster worked together to create an interesting and varied examination of a common design element.

below: Artwork by Darlene Wilkinson
opposite: Artwork by Gail Pierce and Valerie Foster

Our character is but the stamp on our souls of the free choices of good and evil we have made through life. Geikie

PAPER BAG
Collaborative

THIS COLLABORATIVE ART JOURNAL WAS DONE AS AN EXCHANGE AND ASSEMBLED by Michelle Remy. The work is cleverly housed in a book made of paper bags. Almost all the participants provided originals for everyone else's book in lieu of photocopies, which increases the quality of the results.

cover: Michelle Remy

CREATING A BOOK FROM PAPER BAGS

1. Stack paper bags on top of each other, alternating the open end from left to right with each additional paper bag. The openings form a pocket in which you can place pages, artist information, or other goodies.

2. Fold the bags in half, forming a spine.

3. Sew a straight line up the center of the fold.

4. If you would like, you can decorate the binding edge. Try tying a ribbon or sewing on ephemera such as a twig, an artificial flower, a small paintbrush—whatever suits the book's contents. Additionally, you can fold the book and add eyelets, brads, ribbons, or a metal binding clip about a half inch in from the folded edge.

below: From left, work by
Catherine Van der Hoff,
Dawn Sellers, and Linda Duffy

bottom: From left, work by
Sandra Müller, Maggie Tomei,
and Marian Savill

top: From left, work by Kari Gibson, Liz Gale, and Tami Roth

above: From left, work by Ellen Specht and Angela Jarecki

THE PAPER WHIMSY
Alphabet Soup Collaborative

WITH THE ALPHABET SET AS A TOPIC TO EXPLORE, *ALPHABET SOUP* SEEMED a natural title. Campbell's Soups even granted permission for the original cover artwork. A special cover was created for use in this book to avoid trademark infringement issues.

above: Paper Whimsy's new
Alphabet Soup cover

artist: Rande Hanson's letter "A"

artist: Joanna Pierotti's letter "T"

artist: Gale Blair's letter "H"

artist: Debby Harriettha's letter "F"

artist: Bev Froese's letter "W"

artist: Theresa Martin's letter "X"

artist: Lou McCulloch

artist: Caren McNee

artist: Sally Turlington

artist: Katie Kendrick

artist: Dawn Supina

artist: CeCe Grimes

ALTERED BOOK ROUND ROBINS

THE FUN OF ALTERING AN EXISTING BOOK INTO AN ART-FILLED TREASURE IS OFTEN BEST SHARED. ALTERED BOOK ROUND ROBINS ABOUND, AND SEVERAL YAHOO GROUPS EXIST SIMPLY FOR THIS PURPOSE.

Sometimes the participants work with the theme of the book being circulated, and sometimes the participants work the theme into the book regardless of the book's content. Either way, the book structure provides a great stepping-off point for collaboration.

One dilemma that books can face when they are altered is that they become too thick. One way to address this issue is to choose a book with a sewn—rather than glued—binding and remove some pages from each signature (the sewn-in groups of pages) or remove entire signatures.

Sturdier work surfaces can be created by gluing groups of pages together. Using a permanent glue stick rather than a more liquid-type glue will reduce paper wrinkling. If the book is used to work a theme that is not related to the actual content of the book, many artists coat the page surfaces with gesso.

If your book is older, you will want to consider reinforcing the binding. A book traveling in a round robin gets a great deal of handling and shipping. An easy way to reinforce the binding is to first cover the outside of the spine with fabric. Then cover the crease inside the book covers where the text block (the total collected pages) meets the book cover boards with an approximately 4" (10.2 cm) -wide strip of Tyvek envelope adhered with PVA glue or glue stick. This strip, which extends about an inch or two over the book cover board and an inch or two onto the cover page of the book, provides a strong reinforcement for an older or damaged book. The endpapers can be recovered with decorative paper to hide the reinforcement.

THE ALTERED
Calendar Round Robin

A FASCINATING ALTERED BOOK ROUND ROBIN WAS DONE USING SPIRAL CALENDARS as the book base. The participants had hoped that the spiral binding would leave room for the artwork to expand. In the end, these fat, juicy books leaked artwork so steadily from their bindings that their spiral bindings were removed and replaced with huge binder rings. Some books from this collaborative project are so full of art they simply won't close. Each month, the artists received a new calendar to work in, and many aligned the content of their work with their designated month. Hosted by Kathy Wasilewski, this group was so large that two groups of twelve formed, allowing each participant a full year's pages in which to work.

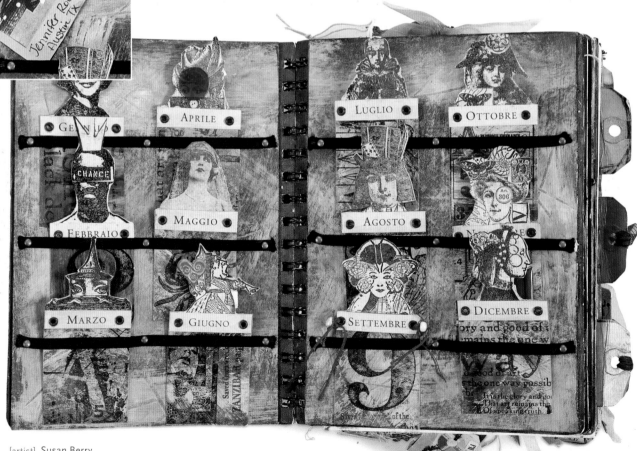

[artist] Susan Berry

exhibit

No. 78

Her grades were good
but not her
ATTENDANCE

artist: Kathy Wasilewski

ALWAYS

BE PATIENT

B

AND

KIND

artist: Lou McCulloch

artist: Kim Logan

artist: Liz Smith

Each artist began her book and set the tone by working in January. The next artist in the mailing order took on February, followed by the remaining months in order. The artists involved were all members of the same large art group that already had a Yahoo group, but to keep lines of communication clear, they formed a separate Yahoo group.

A few road bumps occurred along the way when one person dropped out early and another kept the book she had. But given the size of the group and the volume of mailings (some across the globe), it went fairly well. Because the Yahoo group made it easy to stay in contact, members were aware if an artist needed more time in shipping out work or if contact information changed. The members reported overwhelmingly that there was a high level of camaraderie and a number of fast and dear friendships formed.

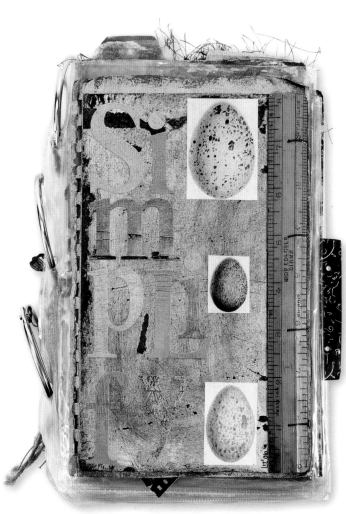

artist: Liz Smith

artist: CeCe Grimes

artist: Claudia Roulier

artist: Jennifer Rowland

artist: Sally Turlington

artist: Marci Glenn

"The Age of Technology has both revived the use of writing and provided ever more reasons for its spiritual solace. Emails are letters, after all, more lasting than phone calls, even if many of them r 2 cursory 4 u."

—ANNA QUINDLEN

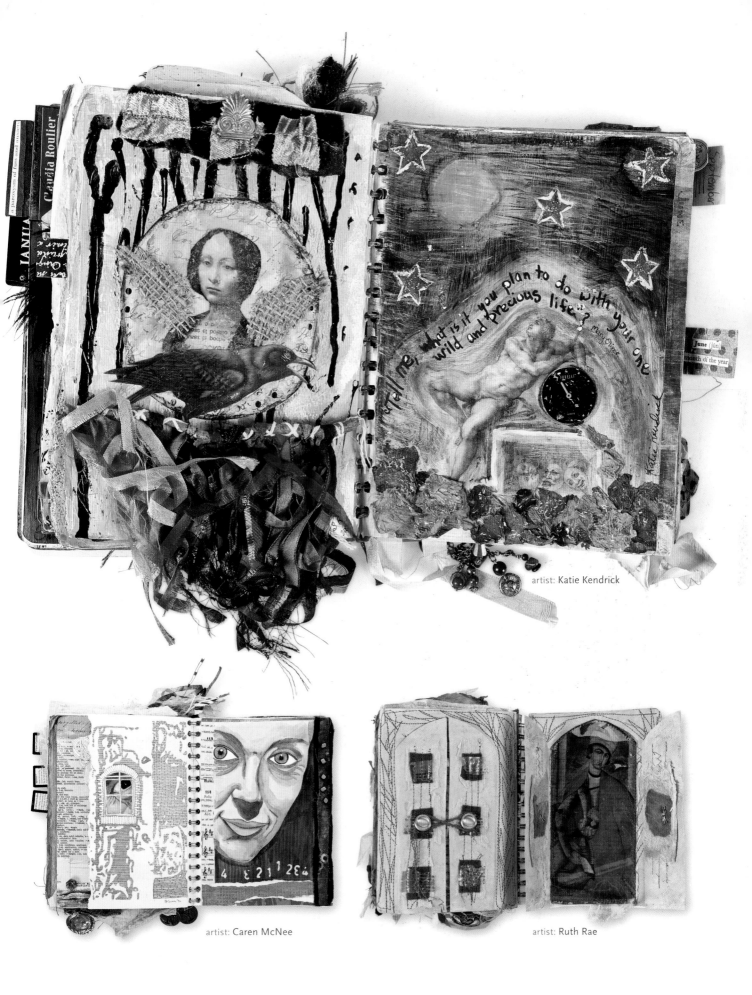

artist: Katie Kendrick

artist: Caren McNee

artist: Ruth Rae

THE HOPE BOOK
Collaborative Project

MELISSA WALKER, A TEACHER AT RANDALL HIGH SCHOOL IN NORTH CAROLINA, invited artists David Modler and Eric Scott of Journal Fodder Junkies in for a workshop for her high school art students. During this workshop, the students and teachers were encouraged to work in this book as a collaborative project. The project had no formal name and no rules.

artist: Josh Loftis

artist: Anna Rice

artist: Mandy Strelko

artist: Tyler Joyner

THE IMPACT OF THE
Internet, email, blogging on us as artists

"Blogging has changed every-thing for me. Being in a somewhat remote part of the country (Montana) I have met very few people who 'get' what I do artistically. Blogging has opened up a whole new avenue of communication and inspiration."

— Jamie Vowel

"I have mixed feelings about it (the Internet). I really enjoy the community, the sharing, the real intimacy and friendships that can grow. People are so generous online and it allows me an opportunity to see so many more kinds of art and artists than I would otherwise. It's also been critical in making, buying, and selling original art accessible to anybody. On the other hand, it can eat up huge chunks of time that could otherwise be spent on art making."

–Tina Abbott

"If it wasn't for the Internet, I wouldn't be an artist or a published writer. All I have done in art and in writing (that is published) came from people and connections I made online. The benefits have outweighed any problems, and the enriching conversations and friends have far outlasted any disappointments over round robins."

— Loretta Marvel

"As for the community of blogging artists, I couldn't live without 'em! Especially lately. I feel like I am just coming into my own as an artist and the love, respect, ooh, ahs, and just general interest I receive through my blog is worth its weight in gold! Of course, there is so much eye candy out there to see, and an endless sea of inspiration, but the women behind the beautiful words and images are the real art. The friendships made in this odd little art-blog world are the real deal. And I am eternally grateful for that. Because that is rare in any setting!"

— Amy

"If it weren't for art (specifically Art & Soul Portland, 2007), I wouldn't be blogging. I'm sure I'm not the only person who hesitated to start a blog because they thought they had nothing in particular to say. But what a kick in the pants it is to get a comment from someone on another continent! As for the Internet and email in general, it's invaluable in keeping track of collaboration details and encouraging fellow artists in the group."

— Lisa Myers Bulmash

"When considering a workshop, I love finding someone has blogged her way through the workshop, day by day, making my decision easy and informed. I love hearing a name and finding his or her work thru Google."

— Ann Bagby

"I think there is a great community of people who are interested in the same things I am. The Internet has opened up the world to all of us artists. I never would have been able to have friends in the UK, Netherlands, and Australia without the Internet. I have never had so many friends that I have never actually met. I met my local art friends through a Yahoo group. My sister was diagnosed with cancer in January and she passed away in May. When this happened, members of my Yahoo group, Mixed Media Art Friends, got together and created a fatbook for me. It is by far the most intimate and personal piece of art that I have ever received. I felt loved like you don't know. I never met any of these women. Yet, they all took the time to do this for me."

— Belinda Spiwak

At ArtFest all the artists are INSPIRED to come out of their cages and run AMOK making it wild and raucous A wonderful...

Circus of Artists

RETREAT
SWAPS

ALL ACROSS THE COUNTRY—AND INDEED THE WORLD—ARTIST ADVENTURES OCCUR IN RETREAT AND CONFERENCE SETTINGS. THESE ART RETREATS PROVIDE A MUCH-NEEDED OPPORTUNITY FOR ARTISTS TO MEET, PARTICIPATE IN WORKSHOPS, ENJOY ACTIVITIES, AND MAKE FRIENDSHIPS.

Many online friendships are cemented at art retreats. Often artists are isolated due to geographic location or the solitary nature of the art-making process, and these venues prove a welcome connection to the other members of their "tribe." Most venues have a Yahoo group set up for communication among attendees and for information from event organizers. From these listservs, retreat-based swaps and exchanges flourish. Participating in retreat-based swaps and exchanges gives people a chance to chat via email about a common topic and provides a nice way for people attending for the first time to begin to forge connections. Information about retreat events can be found in the back matter of most paper arts magazines.

5

opposite: ArtFest Fatbook

THE ARTFEST
Artist Trading Card Swap

ARTIST BEE SHAY ORGANIZES A YEARLY ARTFEST ATC SWAP. ARTFEST IS AN ANNUAL retreat held in Port Townsend, Washington, and organized by Teesha and Tracey Moore. With upwards of 600 attendees, the pool of potential participants is large. More people submit registration materials than the retreat can actually hold, so there is a swell of anticipation preceding the event. At the 2008 event, there was such intense interest in the swap that at distribution time there were long lines filled with excited participants.

Inner-view with Bee Shay

Tell me about the organization of the ATC swap.

Sign-ups open right after ArtFest registration opens. There is a database in the ArtFest Yahoo groups for this purpose. I do not limit the number of participants. Each person sends me twenty-seven ATCs and gets twenty-six in return. The ATCs are returned in book form (pocket pages). The cost to participate covers the cost of producing and shipping the book to ArtFest for distribution. People can join at the last minute or drop out...it's pretty open. Once the deadline has passed, I close the exchange and accept no more entries. You do not have to be attending to

participate. The card form is an ATC (2.5″ × 3.5″ [6 × 9 cm]) and the minimum weight is cardstock or photostock. All twenty-seven cards can be the same or different. Good-quality copies on heavy stock are acceptable.

All originals (similar or different) are acceptable.

What is it like to host such a large swap? How did you keep everything organized?

I love hosting this particular exchange mainly because ArtFest is so near and dear to my heart. It's a bit daunting keeping it organized but I learn more and more each year to make it easier. One of the big perks of doing this is all the people I've met because of it—such a diverse group of interesting people with so much to offer. I also love the fact that it gives festal virgins (people attending for the first time) a real opportunity to jump in and feel the spirit right from the start. It's all a part of what ArtFest is all about—sharing, caring, and giving. A generosity of spirit keeps the creative fires burning.

How long has the ArtFest ATC swap gone on?

This coming year, 2009, will be its fourth consecutive year. I enjoy the sense of community and celebration.

How long have you been working in collaborative projects? Any favorites? What do you enjoy about the collaborative process?

I've been participating in collaborative projects since 1996, and all of them seem to be my favorite. I enjoy the interaction with an online community that blossoms into friendships. Some of them are now among my most important relationships.

[left] Bee Shay, organizer of the ArtFest ATC swap, created this clever ATC-size pocket page book for each swap participant.

*"Every artist in every
medium creates a
personal record of his
social experience."*

—ROBERT DORY

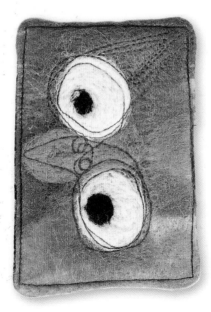

The ArtFest Fatbook

These arty books are ultra-thick and chock-full of arty goodness—hence the designation, fatbook. Fatbooks are a common form of artistic collaboration and are basically the results of an art exchange bound into an impossibly thick book loaded with original art. Pages tend to be no larger than 6″ (15.2 cm) square, and can be made of paper or fabric.

These ArtFest fatbooks were coordinated by Carol Parks for the ArtFest retreat held in 2007. Given the large number of participants, the work involved in coordinating is substantial.

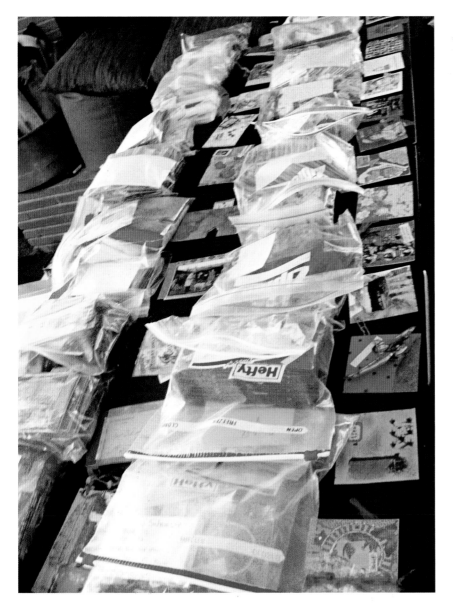

above & left: Stacks of boxes become stacks of pages to be bound into ArtFest Fatbooks at Carol Park's studio.

opposite: More ATC work from the ArtFest 2008 ATC swap

Beauty on the Beach, K.Harcus, 2007

Carte Postale

Notes from one woman's
journey along the path of
Life and Art.
This artist's journey has
begun but there are many
miles yet to travel. There
is no knowing where it
will lead. Join me.

play

Kelly Harcus
Aka Kel or Kel eh
kelspace.typepad.com
Kel_eh@hotmail.com
United Kingdom

of your dreams

wish you were here

where am I?

Fly

soar

Passion

Explore

ART

Adventure

"EACH FRIEND REPRESENTS A WORLD IN US,
A WORLD POSSIBLY NOT BORN UNTIL THEY
ARRIVE, AND IT IS ONLY BY THIS MEETING THAT
A NEW WORLD IS BORN." – Anais Nin

MARCH 28 to APRIL 1
FORT WORDEN STATE PARK
PORT TOWNSEND WASHINGTON

Linda Mondloch, Seattle / lmondloc@mindspring.com

artists: Linda Mondloch (L) and Catherine Witherell (R)

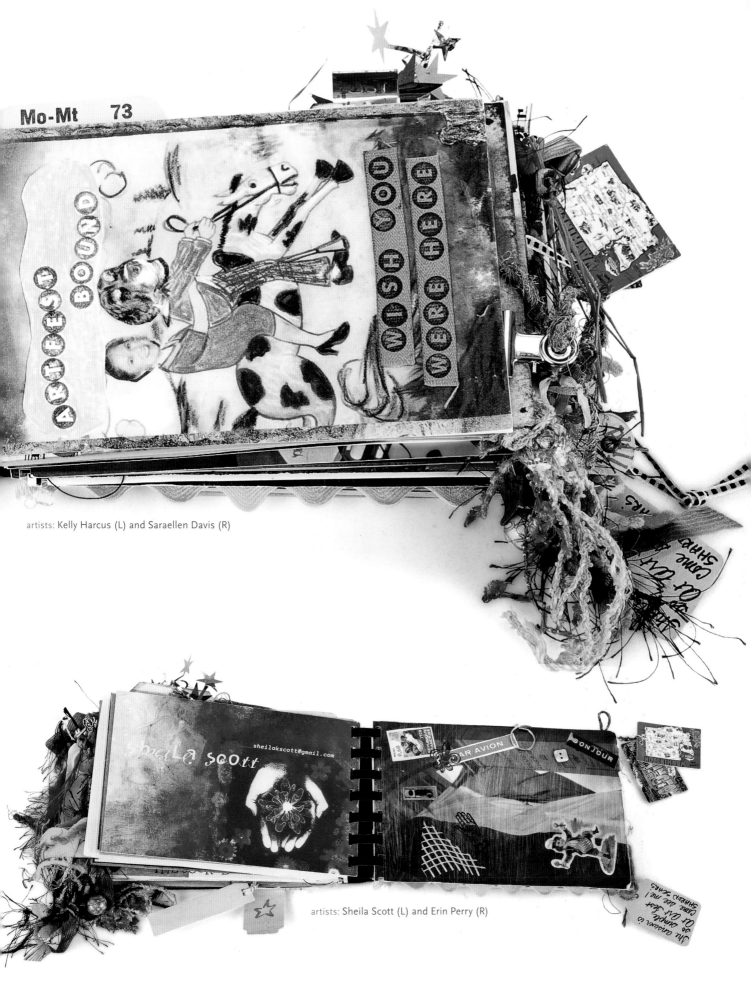

artists: Kelly Harcus (L) and Saraellen Davis (R)

artists: Sheila Scott (L) and Erin Perry (R)

ARTFEST
Fiber Fatbook

WITH SO MANY EXCITED ATTENDEES COUNTING DOWN THE DAYS UNTIL THE event, there is never a shortage of participants for swaps for any of the retreat venues. The ArtFest fiber fatbook, coordinated by Rose Momsen and Saraellen Davis, is literally bursting with enthusiasm. Saraellen describes the process.

APR 02 2008

left: Lilia Meredith's
Spring Secrets collaborative piece,
Sing at the Party, the finished work.

INNER-VIEW WITH SARAELLEN DAVIS

Tell me about the ArtFest fiber fatbook. How did the idea for a fiber fatbook arrive?

My first year attending the ArtFest, someone else hosted the fiber fatbook. The second year, I contacted that person and she was not attending. I asked for volunteers to host and no one stepped up, so I did it, even though I had never hosted anything like that before. By the time the third year ArtFest schedule came out, I already had an idea for the book in mind. I start thinking about the next year's fiber book while I am working on the current year. It's a big job, so last year, the third year, I asked Rose Momsen to help.

Here's what Rose Momsen had to say about joining in on the fun:

She [Saraellen] and I fell in love with the whole idea of doing another one together, across the continent, which was really nuts in practice, but fun to organize via email and cell phone! We had so many ArtFesters in 2008 who wanted to play that we decided to make two books. Some pages were sent to me, some to Saraellen, and some she forwarded on to me for my big Book II Assembly Day. Sara had done a fiber fatbook in 2006 and built on the idea from there. We both create artwork in fiber and so using only fabric appealed to us both. Besides, all of those beads and ribbons and glitsy bits need to go someplace! We plan to do another fiber fatbook for ArtFest 2009, since so many people really liked this version for 2008.

What are the rules for participants?

There are no rules, really! There are just size requirements of 4" × 4"(10 × 10 cm). Depending on how the book will be bound, there is to be nothing on the side of the binding for about 1" (2.5 cm) in from that edge. This will allow for an easy, smooth binding.

The books are assembled beautifully! How do the books get bound?

Each book is bound by hand. There are many different binding techniques, so I choose one that strikes my fancy at that moment. I do think about it all year, and I just want it to be different than the year before.

What's the best part about organizing the ArtFest fiber fatbook?

Meeting all the participants. By the time they pick up their books at ArtFest, I feel like I know everyone already from all the banter back and forth as participants are preparing. And then when handling their individual pages and organizing them for placement in the book, I really get a feel for each person's personality and creativity.

Are you involved in other retreat swaps also?

I am usually involved in some other swap going on at ArtFest as well, as a participant though, not as a host. I have participated in the paper fatbooks, the ATC fatbooks, jewelry swaps, and the never-ending charm swaps. In addition, I am usually involved in other swaps for books or pages on one of the many Yahoo art groups.

What do you enjoy most about working on collaborative art projects?

Saraellen: The finished product! Oh my gosh, they are so beautiful when all completed! And I love seeing the smile on the participants' faces when they pick up their books at ArtFest.

Rose: Not knowing what you'll get in return! The surprise of the return package is what makes collaborative group projects so much fun. We see how happy it has made everyone to have participated in our fatbook project. I have heard that many of the participants really love their books. We had forty-three artists participate, making fifty-seven different pages.

artists: Bee Shay and Jann Sage

artists: Bee Shay and Jann Sage

artists: Marilyn Huskamp and Betty Hooper

A STITCH IN TIME...

...WOULD HAVE CONFUSED EINSTEIN

artists: Sharon K. DuBois, Saraellen Davis, and Rose Momsen

ART EXCHANGES

AN ART EXCHANGE DIFFERS FROM A ROUND ROBIN OR AN ART
JOURNAL COLLABORATIVE BY THE STRUCTURE OF THE PROJECT.
IN AN EXCHANGE, EACH PARTICIPANT SENDS A HOST A SET
NUMBER OF PIECES OF ART IN EXCHANGE FOR A SET NUMBER OF
DIFFERENT PIECES OF ART IN RETURN.

Typically, you submit one more piece than you will receive in return.
An advantage of this kind of collaboration is that regardless of
how many total participants there may be, the number of pieces
any one participant must submit can be kept to a reasonable
level. The person hosting the exchange simply makes sure
that each participant gets a set number of different pieces,
not necessarily one of everything in return. Often the swap
organizer coordinates some special way of compiling the
swap, either in a book, sewn pouch, folder, box, attractive wrap,
or other creative container. Many swap returns contain "goodies"
such as candy or items produced from the artwork, such as buttons,
magnets, tags, or charms, to commemorate the swap.

opposite: Bite-size work from The Art Chix Studio Itty
Bitty Swap

THE CAPOLAN
Exchange

THE GRAND DAME OF PAPER ARTS-RELATED ART EXCHANGES IS CERTAINLY The Capolan Exchange. Based loosely around an idea from one of Nick Bantock's books, The Capolan Exchange has been going for well over a decade. Red Scott is the group's organizer and matriarch.

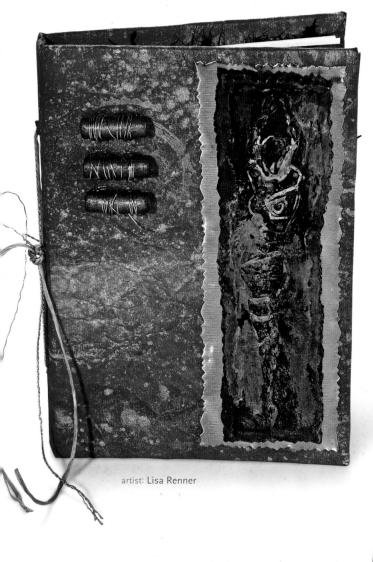

artist: Lisa Renner

artist: Gaye Medbury

INNER-VIEW WITH RED SCOTT

When did the Capolan group exchange begin? How did it come to life?

I put out the invitation for "open media" Capolanesque pieces for August of 1997. At that time, Bantock's *Capolan: Travels of a Vagabond Country Artbox* had just come out and the concept seemed so rich to me. I mean, a vagabond country of people with odd traditions, costumes, and history. It seemed perfect for art concepts and stories.

Is the exchange called The Capolan Caravan?

For seven years, we were known as The Capolan Exchange or The Capolan Caravan. In 2004, I sought to bring in more artists and writers who weren't necessarily seeking to go with the original concept but *were* hoping to find a group they might exchange with that had high standards for submission and dependability as well as artists who enjoyed discussions that included more than the "how to" of any given project. To that end, I opened a group online, called Travelers H'Art, which also included any of the original Capolan Travelers who were still playing.

How many total participants would you guess have traveled with the group?

It would be easier for me to say that in any given month, I have had as few as five players and as many as fifty. Once the online world exploded from the humble "Prodigy" to all the groups one can avail themselves of now, it became much easier to communicate upcoming themes and side projects such as the art decks and other special collaborations. I'd estimate that I've had maybe five hundred artists join us since the exchange's inception.

How many individual works of art would you guess have been generated?

I have twelve boxes of artwork from the exchange "proper" as I think of it. When I say "proper" I'm referring to the advertised Capolan project for any given month, wherein I don't take a sign-up list, I wait and see what comes in. Of the "side excursions," which include the art decks, there are more than fifty decks. We've also done some round robin artists journals, tag projects, and other collaborations. You asked how many individual pieces? I imagine in the high hundreds.

What did Nick Bantock think of the group?

I was invited to meet Nick at a stamp store in Oregon and to bring a suitcase full of works for him to enjoy. He was planning to do a book signing but was going to be stopping at this store first. I have to say, it was a highlight in *this* artist's life to meet the man, and he was absolutely flabbergasted (and more than a little touched) by the tables of inspiration he was made privy to. He had had no idea that his Capolan theme had taken off as it had. I was invited to join Bantock and company for dinner after the book signing and think of that as a magical time.

Does the group use a listserv, email group, or blog to communicate?

Yes. The Capolan website is: www.capolan.org. To find the egroup for getting involved with upcoming projects and discussions, log on to http://groups.Yahoo.com/group/TravelersHart/. Though I'm fairly new to the blogging world I do have one set up now: http://capolan.org/blog/.

What is the actual structure of the exchange, and how does it work?

Typically, I send out invitations through various egroups and note upcoming themes for the exchange on the website. The projects for the now bimonthly exchange can be any media or size, and though they are usually themed, an artist has much more leeway in the choices he or she can make for submission. For those projects, one need only send in her pieces (six for five) by the deadline and include the necessary return postage. The "side" projects, such as the artists' decks, are also organized by invitations and word of mouth. However, for those, I require a sign-up, organize a private egroup for that project only, and communicate the specific guidelines and progress to that group as it goes along.

What sorts of friendships have you developed over the years?

I've made many wonderful friends along the way, some of whom are actually close enough that I can drive over and hang out for an "art play day" when time allows. It's hard in this age, to actually be able to join your friends in the physical realm when so many of them are from all parts of the world. One year, I was able to be at Teesha and Tracy Moore's ArtFest the weekend my birthday fell on. When I got home, I had a surprise waiting for me that several at the event had participated in—The Red Deck. How those folks kept it quiet while I was there, I'll never know! Cath Perkins had initiated the project as a way of thanking me for my efforts, with Keely Barham creating the very cool fabric pouch. There were so many lovely, poignant, and dear sentiments expressed and the artwork, of course, was pretty wonderful as well. Another time, when I was going through the loss of hearing in my right ear, due to a surgery to remove an acoustic tumor, Zoe Hecht stepped up to the plate and solicited a "healing" cards deck project. That one also deeply touched me. So, to answer the question, I feel very blessed to be a part of this community known as The Capolan/Travelers H'Art Exchange.

Any dark moments, such as lost swaps, unusually (unnamed) crazy people, mail gone astray?

Oddly, there have been very few packages that have gone MIA in the postal service. I know of only two wherein I was unable to work out replacements when "returns" went MIA. As for a player's work being lost as it winged its way to me, that has seldom happened as well (that I know of, anyway.) Also, there have been a few times early in the exchange where I felt it necessary to return a player's work, which has earned me a reputation as being somewhat of a "hard sell" hostess. I'm OK with that, since I believe that by protecting one of the stated intents of the exchange (high quality) I've also earned the respect of the players. I'm also happy to note that we've been fortunate not to have had any deeply "troubled" folks show up and try to wreak havoc.

How might you describe the sense of community in the Capolan group?

I have a story about the "community" of the group. In the fall of 2001, we were in the process of wrapping up the annual Halloween art deck project. Then, 9/11 happened. When tragedy strikes, we all, as human beings, want to help in some way, don't we? So when it became clear that there would be a few extra art decks available (due to late dropouts), I inquired of the group, might we auction off the extra decks and donate the funds? I received a unanimous "yes" from the players of that project and I am proud to say that we were able to donate $540 to the Red Cross.

As far as the day to day, there's not a lot of chatter in the egroup. Now and again, a great thread will be started and discussed, and ideas are thrown out for upcoming projects. It's a very safe environment. Though there is a sense that we seek excellence from ourselves, that is not to say that an artist just starting out wouldn't be welcome. They need only be willing to grow and challenge themselves. I'm very proud of the artwork and adore the artists I've come to know through the exchange.

artist: Sandra McCall

artist: Red Scott, Capolan organizer

artist: Annie Onderdonk

artist: Susan Cohen

PURGATORY

artist: Kim Schoen

Capolan
Night Crow

artist: Keely Barham

artist: Amy McClure

COLOR POSTCARD
Exchange

A MONTHLY POSTCARD EXCHANGE IS AN EASY MAIL ART EXCHANGE TO COORDINATE. This particular postcard exchange featured original artworks done using a variety of media, including small paintings, watercolors, sketches, calligraphy pieces, collages, and photographic manipulations. The artists created around a monthly theme or topic, often a color. This allowed artists from the United States and New Zealand, whose work spanned a wide variety of media, to participate. The participants completed nine or ten original postcard-size works and mailed them monthly. These one-of-a-kind postcards provided the recipient artists with an interesting smattering of art and inspiration arriving in their mailboxes monthly, without incurring costly postage expenses.

Postcards exchanged with a blue-gray theme clockwise from top left:
Adriane Giberson,
Pamelia Thomas,
Adriane Giberson,
Pamelia Thomas

Postcards exchanged, inspired by the
color red
clockwise from top left: Debbie Poole,
Adriane Giberson,
Pamelia Thomas, Mary Godfrey

THE ARTCHIX STUDIO
Itty Bitty Swap

HELGA STRAUSS of ARTchix STUDIO COORDINATED THIS EXCHANGE OF ITTY-BITTY, 3" (7.5 cm) square collages, which was also a contest with prizes.

INNER-VIEW WITH HELGA STRAUSS

Tell me about the structure of your exchange.

For this swap, we had approximately fifty participants. The rules were to create six 3" (7.5 cm) square collages with at least one piece of ARTchix Studio faux postage on each collage.

The artists sent in gorgeous collages! I've included a few here. I selected my favorites from all of the collages that were sent in and turned them into a gorgeous collage sheet collection that we now have for sale on our website. I also selected a winner and she received an ARTchix complete faux postage collection. We also had honorable mentions who received a selection of faux postage sheets.

In the end, each participant received the following (which was wrapped up in pretty pink tissue and looked divine.):

above: Shown actual size

* Six collages from different artists in the swap
* The gorgeous collage sheet collection that was created from the swap artwork
* Cute 1" (2.5 cm) buttons that I made (one of the winner's artwork and one of my pieces)
* Yummy chocolate

THE HOLIDAY
Cookbook Exchange

THIS SWEET LITTLE HOLIDAY EXCHANGE WAS ORGANIZED BY GINA ARMFIELD as a fun activity on the Artjournalz Yahoo group.

artist: Holiday Cookbook
organized by Gina Armfield

artist: Gina Armfield

Pop Pop Rossi's Biscotti

These are not the traditional biscotti that you usually see – they are soft and glazed and are an old Sicilian recipe.

Ingredients
5 cups flour
1 cup sugar
4 tsp baking powder
4 eggs beaten
1 cup oil
1oz lemon or anise extract
1 tsp vanilla
½ cup milk

Icing
Confectioner's Sugar
lemon juice or water
(enough to make flowing icing)

Combine dry and liquid ingredients separately. Mix together by adding dry ingredients to incorporated. Knead. On greased pan form dough balls. Bake at 375 degrees light brown. When cookies are still warm spoon icing on top and

Thanksgiving

Quincy House,
Boston, Mass. '99

Oscar G. Barron, Prop'r.

artist: Ginny Ballou

artist: Maija Lepore

MARILYN HUSKAMP'S
Inchie Swaps

THE INCHIES SWAPS THAT ARTIST AND TEACHER MARILYN HUSKAMP COORDINATES began as a retreat swap for ArtFiberFest 2007, and quickly grew more frequent. There are several exchanges a year now. Insiders like to refer to them as "INchies".

INNER-VIEW WITH MARILYN HUSKAMP

Tell me about The House of Friendship collection of inchies.

This swap was organized when we were attending ArtFiberFest 2007. There was no particular theme except to make a 1" × 1" (2.5 × 2.5 cm) fiber inchie. All inchies were mailed to me, and then I coordinated the swap. Each inchie was so unique and beautiful that I couldn't see placing them all in a plastic bag and handing them out to everyone. The inchies seemed to speak to me in a creative way, letting me know that they should be displayed so each artist could see all the creations at a glance and enjoy their beauty. Since home creates happy thoughts of sharing love, I thought, "What better way to display the inchies than a House of Friendship? It will have a warm, giving feeling." Thus the process of constructing the house began.

The number of inchies determined the size of the house. Also, I wanted a way to have the inchies displayed so that they could be removed for use in other artistic creations. I only had tulle, so I used that for the pockets. After trying various colors for the background, I decided to use black, because it created a background that accented the various colors, designs, and patterns. The motto for the house was "Friendships made inch by inch."

How did the other inchie swaps come about?

Spring, my favorite time of year, was the inspiration for the Joy of Spring swap. This needed to be a very special display for everyone. It had to be one that provided a unique, beautiful way to enjoy the artistic creations and accent the inchies in a special way.

"Make a bouquet!" I decided. This would provide a lovely way to show off the small pieces of artwork.

I love working with silk flowers and am always looking for ways to use them in my art. I decided they should be used for the swap. Each silk flower was carefully disassembled. Coordinating ribbons were selected and pockets were sewn onto the ribbons to hold the inchies. The flowers were reassembled with the ribbons under their petals. Once they were all completed, they made a beautiful arrangement.

The Valentine swap is assembled like a fabric type of Valentine's Day card with pockets. Red, pink, and purple dominate the palette, so they became the basis for the card. Clear vinyl was used to make the pockets.

The For My Love of Country inchie swap was inspired by Independence Day. To me, the star signifies hope. I decided to make it the basis for the display. Love of our country has a special meaning to each person in a different way. I wanted to remember and honor those who have fought for our country in past and present wars. The black ribbon honors prisoners of war and the yellow represents faith that those currently at war will return safely. The thirteen pockets are in memory of the beginning, when our country had thirteen states united. Each person's inchie is unique in representing the simplicity and depth of the love felt for our nation. These tiny works of art are but a small symbol of the talents and giving nature the artists incorporate into their creations. I wanted this to be something they could hang up and enjoy.

both: Inchie swap hosted by
Marilyn Huskamp

Friendships made Inch by Inch

REDUCTION CARVING
and Multiblock Carving Technique Swap

Kerrin Conrad hosted this swap, organized through a group called The Carving Consortium. The Carving Consortium is an international group that has been active since 1997. This was a swap based on learning or demonstrating techniques called reduction carving and multiblock printing; there was no designated theme. Artists were to choose a technique and submit the required number of original prints. Each participant received a book of limited-edition hand-printed art.

Reduction carving is a technique in which the artist creates a limited number of art prints from carving one block. The artist begins with carving the first part of the design and then stamping it in the lightest color. Then, the artist carves more of the image, and then stamps the carved block on top of the first image in a darker color. The same happens with the third and subsequent color layers until the composition is complete, resulting in a reduction carved art print.

Multiblock carving is virtually the same as the reduction carving technique except that the artist uses multiple blocks to create a design. Each block represents a color layer in the design.

artist: Susan Denker

"BiG CiTy" ¹⁴/₁₈ U. ROBERTS 2008

FLORIDA PANTHER
Puma concolor coryi

This Puma is another in my series of endangered big cats. It is one of more than twenty subspecies of cougar (Puma concolor). Until 1993 the puma was classified in the genus Felis, along with the domestic cat, the ocelot, and 27 other species. In 1993 the cougar was reassigned to the genus Puma. The subspecies name coryi comes from naturalist/hunter Charles Barney Cory, who first described the panther as a subspecies of cougar. He named it Felis concolor floridana but floridana had already been used for a subspecies of wildcat, so the name was changed to Felis concolor coryi then changed again.

Concolor means one color. Cougar adults are a uniform tawny color with lighter fur on their lower chests, belly, and inner legs. Shades of individual animals may vary considerably from grayish to reddish to yellowish. This uniform color conceals them in a variety of settings. Their color often matches the color of the deer they hunt. Cougar kittens are spotted, which helps to camouflage them in the shadows of their den. There are only about 100 of these pumas known to exist today.

FLORIDA PANTHER

Kandy Lippincott 2008

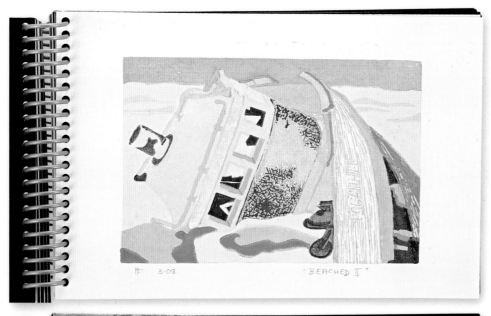

artist: Audrey Fisher

artist: Natasha Hanna

artist: Kerrin Conrad

artist: Julie Hagan Bloch

Julie Hagan Bloch   1.18.2008

"Monsterously Good Friends"

artist: Pam McVay

artist: Donna Back

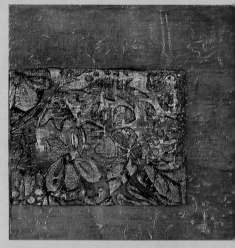

PROJECT EIGHT

FEBRUARY 2008

RED

COLLABORATIVE MIXED-MEDIA EXCHANGES

OBVIOUSLY, NOT ALL COLLABORATIVE ART PROJECTS ARE DONE BY ARTISTS WHO WORK WITH PAPER OR FABRIC. AN AMAZING ARRAY OF THREE-DIMENSIONAL ITEMS ARE WORKED ON BY GROUPS OF ARTISTS. SCULPTURES, ASSEMBLAGES, PAINTINGS, AND BOXES ARE SOME OF THE MORE COMMONLY USED OBJECTS. A SMATTERING OF NON-BOOK MIXED-MEDIA COLLABORATIONS ARE SHOWN IN THIS CHAPTER.

When a collaborative project involves objects such as sculptures or other heavier items, additional consideration must be given to packing materials and shipping costs. Shipping with foam peanuts and shredded paper may be merely messy for shipping an item to a single destination, but shipping from artist to artist requires some creative packing techniques. Air bags and loosely bagged foam peanuts or shredded paper contain the mess without the weight of newspaper or kraft paper padding. Assistance from staff at a shipping store can help make sure your package makes its journey safely.

"Every person has a second date of birth, and one which is more frequent than the first: that on which he discovers what his true vocation is."

—BRASSI

PERSONAL ALLOTMENT:
A Self-Portrait Project

This printer's drawer was worked into an assemblage by artists Carol Kemp, Syd McCutcheon, and Mary Price. As part of a subset of a larger collaborative project called *Three*, Art from Scrap Gallery, curators Holly MacKay and Dug Uyesaka invited ten artists, who, in turn were to each ask two more artists to collaborate with them on a piece of work, forming ten artistic trios. This piece, *Personal Allotment*, had the theme of self-portrait.

MIDNIGHT IN THE VALLEY
OF THE BONES, *an Assemblage, Sculpture, and Jewelry Collaborative*

JEN WORDEN AND DERYN MENTOCK WORKED TOGETHER ON THIS LARGE COLLABORative piece that traveled between Texas, USA, and Nova Scotia, Canada. The idea was to create a melding of mediums, an assemblage that contained a jewelry piece that could be removed and worn. The inspiration for this piece is the Bible story of Ezekiel, who resurrects a valley full of dry bones.

Inner-view with Deryn Mentock

How did the two of you come to collaborate?

I had admired Jen's work and been reading her blog for quite some time. When the idea came to create a piece of jewelry that would also be a part of an assemblage, I immediately thought of Jen. She's one of my favorite assemblage artists—she's extremely inventive and talented. I knew our work would complement each other's very well.

What do you think artists gain by collaborating?

I had been thinking about this piece and had considered doing an assemblage of my own but I really wanted this to be a collaborative project. I felt that collaboration would bring so much more to the work. I typically work alone in my studio with little or no outside input during the creative process. Collaborating with Jen was great because it allowed us both to bounce ideas back and forth, which spawned new ideas. Also, the project went very smoothly, so there was a lot of encouragement and support there.

Tell me how it was you came to choose the story about Ezekiel.

I had studied this story in Ezekiel, chapter 37, and was fascinated by the thought of Ezekiel coming into the middle of a valley of dry bones. When God commanded Ezekiel to speak to the bones, there was a noise and they were covered with flesh but not alive. It was a thrilling moment when God put breath into them and all those bones rattled back to life! I started to think about what it must have been like for Ezekiel in that valley and began to form an idea for a jewelry piece that would include things he might have found during his time there. I love the meaning behind the story—the dry bones represent the people, whose

hope is gone, and God restores them back to life. Jen's assemblage was the perfect complement to the story and the jewelry piece.

Tell me more about the symbolism in the piece.

The elements of the necklace include things that Ezekiel might have encountered in the valley of the bones, such as bones, shells, feathers, coral, stones, and petrified wood. In the chain are chunks of tumbled carnelian, representing a layer in the foundation of heaven and also reminiscent of the flesh and blood covering the bones. There are twelve interchangeable vials that are also filled with things from the valley: seedpods, sand, dirt, sticks, bones, leaves, feathers, shells, and similar items. Two of the vials are filled with objects that represent new life and restoration—the butterfly wing and the eggshells.

The assemblage is in keeping with the overall ancient feel of the piece. On the head is what can be interpreted as a crown of thorns, but it also has the feel of an ethnic headpiece. The focal point of the necklace (the skull) hangs directly down the figure's forehead. The drawer opens and contains the extra vials for the necklace, which can be switched out.

JOURNEYS BOX
Collaboration

THE JOURNEYS BOX COLLABORATION IS HOUSED IN A BOX HANDMADE BY PATRICIA Remington. Her box, which has her poem on the cover and her artwork lining the interior, also houses work by artists Robin Joy Katz, Cami Smith, Laura Mosher, and Anne Marie Colwell. Patricia tells me, "Our group has thirteen artists. The rules for the Journeys journal were best summed up by the cover poem, on the opposite page. We meet once a month and everyone's journal has a different theme to follow, so this is only one of thirteen journals in progress."

[artist] Patricia Remington

[artists] Robin Joy Katz

[artist] Cami Smith

Life's continuing journeys ...
Places that touched your heart
Exotic sights and sounds
Or a feel-good hometown visit

Perhaps a personal journey
Painful or joyous
A time remembered

A newfound love
An exposure to new lands and people
A world of culinary delights
An eagerness to explore and learn
A history of architecture, cities and transit

Remembering past journeys
Dreaming of future ones to be ...

[artist] Laura Mosher

MAGPIE ARTS
Creative Journey Deck

DEB LEWIS COORDINATED A SWAP IN WHICH THE ARTISTS CREATED A SET OF ALTERED playing cards housed in some sort of structure. The surface of the artist-made cards would act as a small canvas. The idea was that much of the art for swaps was done for others and very few pieces of work get retained. The fifty-two cards in a deck were assigned to a week of the year. Each card had to be at least twice as large as a standard playing card, which offered a nice change from doing ATCs. Each artist took a different approach in creating her deck and in creating the subsequent display housing, varying from embellished cigar boxes, display stands, and handmade books. Participants spoke glowingly about the positive environment created by working on a project in a group but making the art to be kept for oneself instead of it being received by another artist.

artist: Kris Henderson

artist: Marcy Hudziak

artist: Christine Shebroe

artist: Deb Lewis

WHO'S YOUR DADDY?
Collaborative Doll Project

IN MARCH 2007, THE SEED FOR *Who's Your Daddy?* GERMINATED FROM A LUNCH date with artists Lynne Sward, Peggy Beardslee, and Elsa Wachs who wanted to do a fiber project together. Here's what Lynne Sward had to say:

"Peggy Beardslee was one of the original three in starting this collaboration. When we all met [the nine other artists, the tenth lives in Philadelphia] we were talking about Anna Nicole Smith and her newly born daughter and the scuttlebutt about who the father was. Peggy said the discussion was so funny because her brother was writing a journal for his family and its title was '*Who's Your Daddy?*' We all exclaimed, 'What a great title for our collaboration!' and thus the name stuck. That phrase was one I remembered from a recent Angelina Jolie/ Brad Pitt movie called *Mr. and Mrs. Smith*. During one of the fight scenes between them, Angelina pins Brad down, and blurts out, 'Who's your daddy now?'"

Inner-view with Lynne Sward and Other Members of the Project

What was the structure of the collaborative process?

The *Who's Your Daddy?* Collaborative Doll Project was completed by ten artists who created ten artistic elements on ten different dolls.

A nine-month timeline, appropriate for the birth of their creations, was established thanks to artist Ray Hershberger, who conceptualized a *Who's Your Daddy?* grid. The grid provided a monthly "round robin" timeline for each doll, detailing which artist was responsible for creating which body part. The only rules were to create after seeing the doll, because the doll would "tell each artist what was needed," and that nothing could be changed or altered on each doll until each was returned to its rightful owner.

To get started, each artist assembled a torso of his or her own chosen media and design. Beverly Furman's doll, Willow, has armature made from flexible willow branches and was fashioned with cotton paper pulp and wood chips. Pamela Winslow drew upon her theater background to create her doll's layered decorative torso.

Each collaborative doll is layered with personality, rich with creative nuance and artistic technique. Artists sewed, sculpted, sawed, sanded, beaded, glued, and painted to produce their vision. These intricacies give breath to each doll, telling the story of its journey and giving insight into each artist. In one imaginative example, Hershberger, inspired by a doll's multicultural details, fashioned a Torah-like scroll for the doll's face, which turns to unveil fifty-three alter egos.

"I had resolved to spend a lot of time thinking about the design for my doll, but a persistent little spirit kept flitting and buzzing around my head, demanding my attention," says Winslow. "I finally gave up and created this pesky muse. It doesn't have a name...free spirits don't have names. It is androgynous...free spirits don't have genders."

Handcrafted journals accompanied each doll's journey from artist to artist, establishing the philosophy and personality of each doll in order to guide the other artists in their work. Monthly, the dolls were passed to the next designated artist to add head, face, arms, legs, feet, hands, hair, clothing, or accessories.

"As each package came to me, I eagerly unwrapped the doll, taking a quick look and then putting the doll away until I had a nice block of time to add my part. As an artist who is interested in craftsmanship and unity, I tried to ensure that whatever I added to each doll was coordinated in color and sensibility to the doll's persona," says Sward.

Lynne Sward reflects on what the experience was like:

"This collaboration was very different for me from others throughout the years, because everyone was from the same vicinity. We were all professional artists, and three males were included," says Sward. "No one other than myself had ever created an art doll. I got a tremendous kick out of seeing the diversity and creativity among the group. How everyone interpreted each doll and decided what that particular doll 'needed' was very exciting and inspiring. It was important to stick to some strong guidelines, such as meeting the monthly deadline, which in some instances had to be extended. When the dolls were exhibited and the public came and saw them, the positive comments and wonderment were overwhelming. The public was indeed fascinated.

From my own perspective and that of others that I talked to (including Peggy), the whole experience was one of growth, experimentation, and fun. Most of the time, we went out of our own comfort zones to

artist: Peggy Beardslee

add our personal touch on each doll. We also had to use restraint and respect, and put our own biases in check while working on the dolls. Peggy and some of the other artists are continuing the doll-making process for future exhibitions. Doll-making is a total blast for me, and I'm constantly looking for new, untried ways of creating one-of-a-kind figurative sculpture."

As the idea took wings, ten artists, working in diverse media, joined the collaboration: Lynne Sward (mixed media), Peggy Beardslee (mixed media), Elsa Wachs (fiber), Ray Hershberger (painting), Linda Gissen (sculpture), Beverly Furman (painting), Matthew Bernier (puppeteer), Pamela Winslow (mixed media), and Barbara and Fred Mason (jewelers).

"This doll project has afforded me the opportunity to work collaboratively with a group of incredibly talented, imaginative artists whose media and artistic visions go in very different directions from my own. It has been both delightful fun and a challenge to work within my own genre to create doll segments that fit within the conceptual vision of the doll's originator," reflects Gissen.

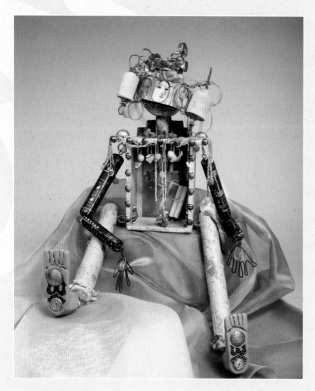

artist: Lynne Sward

artist: Matthew Bernier

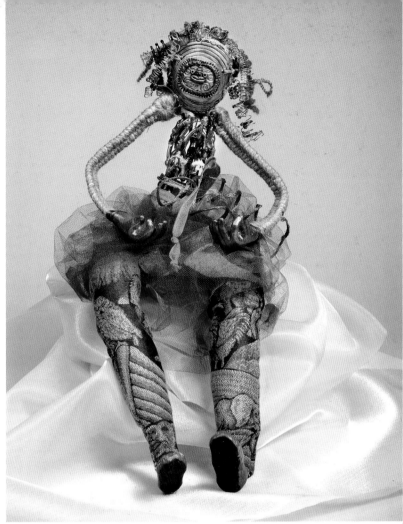

clockwise from left: Art dolls by
Ray Hersheberger, Linda Gissen,
Beverly Furman, and Fred Mason

PROJECT 8
Collaboration

Leighanna Light describes the inception of Project 8 on the group's communal blog: "Each year around this time [mid-December] I seem to cook up some kind of community or collaborative project for the upcoming year. In 2006, I started a group called 'one week at a time,' where a group of local women made one piece of art every week for an entire year. We met once a month to share our work, and at the end of the year we had a group show at a local gallery. It was such a wonderful experience in so many ways. I wanted to do something similar this year, only a little less intense, and expand it to beyond Albuquerque. I was talking with a friend about this one day and she came up with the idea of inviting eight artists to create one 8″ × 8″ (20 × 20 cm) piece of artwork every month for eight months, ending with a show here on the eighth month. I loved the idea. The group filled almost instantly, but there were a few other women who I really wanted to work with. So I decided to do a sister project. The concept of eights was the same, but this collaboration included only out-of-state artists and culminated with a traveling show at the end of eight months. I sent out invitations and almost immediately everyone wrote back and committed to the project."

Project 8
January
2008
Mandala

Inner-view with Project 8 Member Catherine Witherell

What is the construction of the collaboration?

Our collaborative project is called Project 8. It lasts for eight months and has eight participants. The artists are Leighanna Light, Judy Wise, Katie Kendrick, Diane Haven-Smith, Stephanie Lee, Albie Smith, Laurie Mika, and myself. We do eight pieces of art and the rules are simply that the measurements have to be 8" × 8" (20 × 20 cm). The artwork can be from any medium, and each artist picks the theme for a specific month and is responsible for posting the instructions on the "Project 8" blog found at http://project-eight.blogspot.com.

How does the group interact?

We interact by blog post to describe the theme, to show what we have done, and to comment on the work. We also interact by email if there is a long personal story that inspired the theme.

How has Project 8 developed as a group? Is there a feeling of connectedness, of community?

We get to be exposed to the other styles of art, and get an understanding of what drives each artist and why she makes art. For me, I have decided to learn as much as I can from these other wonderfully experienced artists and it is fueling my energy to hone my skills as a mixed-media artist in my own right. I've met everyone but Albie and I am taking a class with her in October 2008.

What other sorts of themes are you pondering?

Themes and their originators are:

* January: Catherine; mandela
* February: Leighanna; red
* March: Laurie; herald spring
* April: Diane; ancestors
* May: Judy; animal dreams
* June: Stephanie; lay me down
* July: Katie; a season in my heart
* August: Albie; if I could go anywhere I'd go to ...

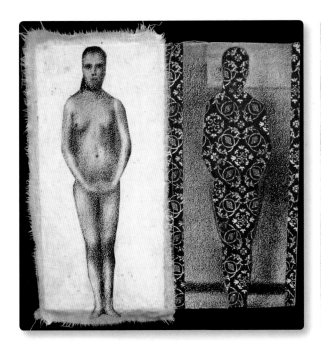

amuerte nos deus sa

Herald Spring

Spring still makes spring in the mind
    When sixty years are told:
Love wakes anew this throbbing heart
    And we are never old.
Over the winter glaciers
    I see the summer glow,
And through the wild-piled snowdrift
    The warm rosebuds below.
RALPH WALDO EMERSON

*"The Internet is becoming the town square
    for the global village of tomorrow."*

—BILL GATES

READER INVITATION

Join our online collaboration! Meet us over on Flickr to share your submission in the collaborative art journal group. We look forward to seeing your work. Ongoing activities are planned, so stop by often: www.flickr.com/photos/collaborativeartjournals

TELL US YOUR STORY ...
Visually!

The topic for our online collaboration is the idea of a visual story. Share your visual story on an 8½" × 11" (21.6 × 27.9 cm) surface of your choosing. The use of text is completely optional, so you can use words or leave them off altogether. Your story can be a small take, a grand story, a day's events, a gothic romance, a mystery, a fairy tale, a biography, a parable, an allegory, the results of a night of dreaming—a story of any shape or size, as long as it fits onto your 8½" × 11" (21.6 × 27.9 cm) surface! Scan or photograph your image and post it to our flickrgroup.

So come and walk awhile with me and share the twisting trails and worlds wonderous Ive known. But this bridge will only take you halfway there. The last few steps you have that to take the alone.

2006 NOVEMBER NOVEMBER NOVEMBRE NOVIEMBRE NOVEMBRE NOVEMBRO NOVEMBER

this is my Nana

Nana's Birthday
(13)

She turns 85 — Wow Still going Strong!

She was always poised on the pinnacle of a drama, a problem, a conflict

13 has always been her LUCKY number... She has always considered herself mystical...

Look how PRETTY! It's a new stamp I just got - part of a sheet of beautiful design elements from Purple Onion Also found this Great Old version of "Lassie"- It's about a man stuck in a well - surprise surprise! Why were they always falling in the well first time she... back then? ha ha

Now Timmy heard the call for help again. He couldn't see anyone below, but he knew that Lassie would find whoever it was in trouble. And maybe he had better see if he could help, too.

WEEK 46

Artwork from the altered *Calendar Round Robin* by Marci Glenn

PROJECT INDEX

CONTRIBUTOR LIST

CINDY ALEXANDER
calex22001@yahoo.com

JULIE ANNE ALLEN
jdancinghorse@gmail.com

CATHERINE ANDERSON
cathy@catherineanderson
studio.com

GINA ARMFIELD
g.armfield@yahoo.com

GINNY BALLOU
ginnyballou@yahoo.com

KEELY BARHAM
fabfrogdesigns@aol.com

CARLA BARRETT
carla.s.barrett@sbcglobal.net

PEGGY BEARDSLEE
textileartist2000@yahoo.com

DIANE BECKA
becka@cnw.com

BINKY BERGSMAN
binky.bergsman@verizon.net

MATTHEW BERNIER
portsartist@yahoo.com

SUSAN BERRY
fiverdog@dsl.pipex.com

ROCHELLE BETTIS
RB@photographybyrochelle.
com

DONNA BLACK
artsnacker@artsnacker.com

JODEE BLACK
jodee.black@yahoo.com

GALE BLAIR
beau@paperwhimsy.com

KIM BOEHM
dogfairies5@yahoo.com

ANDREW BORLOZ
cooknfold@aol.com

JOY BROOKS
joyb87544@yahoo.com

ELIZABETH BUNSEN
planetbone@comcast.net

KATHY CAMERON
kathcam123@hotmail.com

DONNA CARTAGENA
gyspyart1@earthlink.net

SUSAN COHEN
slcstamps@yahoo.com

JULIE COLLINGS
juliecollings2003@hotmail.
com

ANNE MARIE COLWELL
annemariecolwell@yahoo.com

KERRIN CONRAD
conradclub@aol.com

GAIL COWAN
runmoremiles@comcast.net

CONNIE COX
tandccox1@comcast.net

CYNTHIA CURTIS
curtiscynthia@hotmail.com

COLLEEN DARLING
colleen950@gmail.com

SARAELLEN DAVIS
blubyu1957@yahoo.com

GWEN DELMORE
gwennie52@hotmail.com

SUZANNE DENKER
sdenker@hotmail.com

DEB DENTON
endlssmmer@yahoo.com

KECIA DEVENEY
keeshagirl4@aol.com

SHARON K. DUBOIS
skdubois@yahoo.com

PEGGY DUFFNER
pegette1@yahoo.com

LINDA DUFFY
lindaduf@mchsi.com

ALINA EDRY
alinaedry@hotmail.com

MARIA FAZIO
mbf5@verizon.net

RANDI FEUERHELM-WATTS
randifw@gmail.com

ANNE FISHER
annie.b.f@comcast.net

AUDREY LOUISE FISHER
abanczyk@cfl.rr.com

VALERIE FOSTER
vjdoc83@yahoo.com

BEV FROESE
bevfroese@gmail.com

BEVERLY FURMAN
beverlyfurman@earthlink.net

LIZ GALE
lzgale@aol.com

ADRIANE GIBERSON
Adriane@onesundayafternoon.
com

LAURIE GIBERSON
giberson@winfirst.com

KARI GIBSON
karolinagibson@btinternet.
com

TAMMY GILLEY
tammy@tammygilley.com

CINDY GILSTRAP
cindy.gilstrap@prodigy.net

LINDA GISSEN
info@lindagissen.com

MARCI GLENN
mglenn@integrity.com

MARY GODFREY
kandart@sbcglobal.net

SARAH GREENER
exp510@aol.com

CECE GRIMES
cece627@comcast.net

LORI GUERIN
lmguerin@twcny.rr.com

JULIE HAGAN BLOCH
juliehaganbloch@hvc.rr.com

NATASHA HANNA
junaha@verizon.net

MARGOT HANSON
margotlouhanson@hotmail.
com

RANDE HANSON
R2Art.Studio@yahoo.com

KELLY HARCUS
kels.email@gmail.com

DEBBY HARRIETTHA
tomndeb@sympatico.ca

DIANE HAVEN-SMITH
diane@innerstandings.com

KRIS HENDERSON
kriskhenderson@gmail.com

CHRISTINE HENDRY
roguech@yahoo.com

JANET HERITAGE
planet2janet2003@yahoo.com

RAY M. HERSHBERGER
hershberger@virtualperal.net

NELDA HINDS
nelhinds@yahoo.com

BETTY HOOPER
bchooper@yahoo.com

LYNNE HOWE
lynne.howe@yahoo.co.uk

MARCY HUDZIAK
MHudziak@aol.com

JENNY HUNTER GROAT
hermitfarm@earhtlink.net

MARILYN HUSKAMP
marilynsnouvelle@yahoo.com

TRACIE LYN HUSKAMP
thereddoorstudio@yahoo.com

CHRISTINA ISPERDULLI
isperduli@yahoo.com

ANGELA JARECKI
ajarecki@comcast.net

DANA FOX JENKINS
dana.jenkins@roswellpark.org

JUANITA JOHNSON
settlerspeace@verizon.net

MICHELLE JOHNSON
michelle@craftedby.us

TYLER JOYNER
tyler_joyner@yahoo.com

CARINA KARLSSON
elakmor@yahoo.com

ROBIN JOY KATZ
rkatz@cfl.rr.com

CATHY KEITH
cbkeith@roadrunner.com

CAROL KEMP
lifsart@verizon.net

Katie Kendrick
joyouslybecoming@earthlink.
net

Sarah Ketchley
sarah@kitandkaboodledesigns.
com

Ruth Krening
kreningr@gmail.com

Stephanie Lee
stephanielee@q.com

Maija Lepore
leporeazi@cox.net

Deb Lewis
artsydiva@comcast.ent

Leighanna Light
lklight@copper.net

Terrie Lightfoot
lost_art_creations@yahoo.com

J. Kandy Lippincott
kandylippincott@gmail.com

Josh Loftis
loftisjw@appstate.edu

Kim Logan
kim@kimlogan.co.uk

Kathy Lopez
kauaiartgirl@yahoo.com

Delorse Lovelady
loverainsky@yahoo.com

Joe Ludwig
joseph15143@yahoo.com

L.K. Ludwig
ludwiglk@aol.com

Maggie Ludwig

Linda Lyon
lwlyon@wegelyon.org

Linda Mansour
lmm94566@aol.com

Theresa Martin
info@theresamartin.com

Loretta Marvel
artjournal@optonline.net

Barbara Mason
bjburgandy@yahoo.com

Fred Mason
stones.mason@att.net

Sandra McCall
mccallss@commspeed.net

Amy McClure
at1kp2@mchsi.com

Melissa McCobb Hubbell
MMHubbell@earthlink.net

Jacqueline McColl
jackie@artchixstudio.com

Lou McCulloch
loutomedina@zoominternet.
net

Syd McCutcheon
floozy@verizon.net

Connie McDowell
conniemcdowell@comcast.net

Cindy McMath
cindy@artchixstudio.com

Paula McNamee
ppmcnamee@msn.com

Caren McNee
dcmcnee@slingshot.co.nz

Pam McVay
pammcv@comcast.net

Gaye Medbury
stmpbabe@aol.com

Deryn Mentock
mocknet@sbcglobal.net

Lilia Meredith
lilializbet@hotmail.com

Judy Merrill-Smith
cheerytomato@hotmail.com

Laurie Mika
laurie@mikaarts.com

Rose Momsen
geonrose@pointroberts.net

Linda Mondloch
lmondloch@mindspring.com

Diane Moore
enchy@enchylatta.com

Susan K. Moore
anuenuestudio@yahoo.com

Laura Mosher
laura.mosher@gmail.com

Heather Muenstermann
muenstermann_h@yahoo.com

Sandra Müller
Sandra.muller@
theartofconfusion.com

Laura Murray
domanidesigns@yahoo.com

ANNIE ONDERDONK
annie5727@gmail.com

LINDA O'NEILL
fontluvr@aol.com

MARIE OTERO
paperartzi@cs.com

CAROL PARKS
cp@carolparks.com

DEBORAH PAUL
deborah@
darkafternoonprojects.com

ERIN PERRY
erinreneeperry@hotmail.com

DJ PETTITT
jndpettitt@charter.net

GAIL PIERCE
mizriley2003@yahoo.com

JOANNA PIEROTTI
joanna@mosshillstudio.com

DEBBIE POOLE
rpetal1234@aol.com

LYNNE PORTER
lynne.porter@talktalk.com

MARY PRICE
bbb3@cox.net

RUTH RAE
ruthrae@gmail.com

KARI RAMSTROM
kari_ramstrom@visi.com

CAROL REGAN
mooncaroler@yahoo.com

PAT REMINGTON
plremington@earthlink.net

MICHELLE REMY
hand-soul@suddenlink.net

LISA RENNER
lisarenner@tx.rr.com

AMY ELISE ROBERTS
amyeliseroberts@msn.com

VAL ROBERTS
varoberts@aol.com

BETH ROBINSON
pumpkin12pm@gmail.com

KRISTEN ROBINSON
artsyk1@gmail.com

KARLA ROSENDALL
krosendall@gmail.com

TARA ROSS
tlrossco@yahoo.com

TAMI ROTH
mroth@lcom.net

CLAUDIA ROULIER
abobthecat@aol.com

JENNIFER ROWLAND
jmr@ccam.com

JANN SAGE
jsage@hewm.com

MARIAN SAVILL
mazza@savhall.freeserve.co.uk

SHANNON SAWYER
sawyershannon@aol.com

KIM SCHOEN
stampme@cpros.com

RED SCOTT
reddogscott@capolan.org

RHONDA SCOTT
retrorose@rockisland.com

SHEILA SCOTT
sheilakscott@gmail.com

LORI SEAVEY-CHRISTIAN
lori@artandplay.com

DAWN SELLERS
ddsellers@hotmail.com

BEE SHAY
bee.shay@hotmail.com

CHRISTINE SHEBROE
MsCrisy@aol.com

LOUIE SHELLENBERGER
louie@whidbey.net

DAWN M. SHEPHERD
dawn@motherrubber.com

ALBIE SMITH
papersmith@starband.net

CAMI SMITH
smicam@gmail.com

LIZ SMITH
conaltart@yahoo.co.uk

KELLY SNELLING
smallbird@cox.net

APRIL SONCRANT
a_soncrant@yahoo.com

CARLA SONHEIM
carla@carlasonheim.com

WES SONHEIM

BETSEY SPENCER
bk.spencer@comcast.net

DEBRA SPENCER
djwest36@yahoo.com

ELLEN SPECHT
floweress@aol.com

HOLLY STINNETT
hollystinnett@att.net

JULIE STOWE
stowestamp@aol.com

HELGA STRAUSS
helga@artchixstudio.com

MANDY STRELKO
alstrelk@uncg.edu

MEG STURT
margot-mac@hotmail.com

DAWN SUPINA
canada_eh2000ca@yahoo.ca

LYNNE SWARD
610arts38@cox.net

JOANNE THIEME HUFFMAN
thiemehuffman@yahoo.com

PAMELIA THOMAS
pamelia@swbell.net

JILL THOMPSON
jetjill1960@hotmail.com

MAGGIE TOMEI
mftomei@hotmail.com

SALLY TURLINGTON
sallyt1@suddenlink.net

MICHELE R. UNGER
Michele@nwlink.com

CATHERINE VAN DER HOEFF
p.sutmuller@hetnet.nl

MICHELE VASS
vassartima@comcast.net

JAMIE VOWELL
jamievowell@yahoo.com

ELSA WACHS
elsa@elsawachs.com

CASSONDRA WALTERS
cassandbrian@yahoo.com

ARLENE WANETICK
arelenewanetick@comcast.net

KATHY WASILEWSKI
mrswas@comcast.net

RAMONA WEYDE FERCH
rweyde@gmx.net

DARLENE WILKINSON
darlene11@gmail.com

BOONE WILSON
planetboone@comcast.net

PAMELA WINSLOW
pamelawinslow@verizon.net

JUDY WISE
judywise@canby.com

CATHERINE WITHERELL
cathwitherell@comcast.net

ANDREA WOODYATT
specialfx3@aol.com

JEN WORDEN
jen@jenworden.com

RESOURCES

A.C. MOORE
www.acmoore.com

ARCHIVER'S
www.archiversonline.com

THE ART STORE
A BLICK COMPANY
www.artstore.com

CARDBLANKS (Canada and US)
www.cardblanks.com

CHARMED CARDS & CRAFTS
(UK)
www.charmedcardsandcrafts.
co.uk

CHEDDAR STAMPER (UK)
www.cheddarstamper.co.uk

CRAFTS, ETC.
www.craftsetc.com

CREATE FOR LESS
www.createforless.com

CREATIVE CRAFTS (UK)
www.creativecrafts.co.uk

CURRY'S ART STORE (Canada)
www.currys.com

DANIEL SMITH
www.danielsmith.com

DICK BLICK
www.dickblick.com

ECKERSLEY'S ARTS, CRAFTS,
AND IMAGINATION (New South
Wales, Queensland, South
Australia, and Victoria)
www.eckersleys.com.au

FABRIC PLACE
www.fabricplace.com

FLAX
www.flaxart.com

GRAPHIGRO (France)
www.graphigro.com

HOBBYCRAFT GROUP LIMITED
(UK)
www.hobbycraft.co.uk

JERRY'S ART-A-RAMA
www.jerrysartarama.com

JO-ANN FABRICS
www.joann.com

JOHN LEWIS (UK)
www.johnlewis.co.uk

KATE'S PAPERIE
www.katespaperie.com

LAZAR STUDIOWERX INC
(Canada)
www.lazarstudiowerx.com

MAKING MEMORIES
www.makingmemories.com

MEMORY VILLA
www.memoryvilla.com

MICHAELS, THE ARTS & CRAFTS
STORE
www.michaels.com

MOLESKINE
www.moleskine.com

OFFICEMAX
www.officemax.com

PAPER SOURCE
www.paper-source.com

PEARL ART AND CRAFT SUPPLY
www.pearlpaint.com

STAPLES
www.staples.com

TARGET
www.target.com

T N LAWRENCE & SON LTD (UK)
www.lawrence.co.uk

About the Author

L.K. Ludwig creates art and chases her three small children around in a Victorian Foursquare in a small town (pop. 4,023) in western Pennsylvania. Many weekends are spent in the woods and at the river with her husband and her children, where family memories and art are made while the Allegheny River flows by. Because of her strong belief in creating around what she knows, nature, parenting, love, and life seep deeply into L.K.'s artwork, making it content-rich and personally meaningful. She is author of *Mixed-Media Nature Journals* and *True Vision: Authentic Art Journaling*, Quarry Books, 2008. Her artwork has been featured in a number of books, magazines, and galleries. She enjoys teaching at various venues across the United States and internationally.

Acknowledgments

The sheer volume of collaborative work occurring among artists is staggering. It is my privilege to give you this *slimmest* of glimpses into this body of work.

Eleven years ago, I was searching for ways to transform my existing body of work and somehow I stumbled upon an online community through listservs, participating in collaborations and making connections across the globe and forming dear friendships.

Thank you, my littles, Gryphon, Maggie, and Sunny; you fill my days and my heart with joy. Joe, my husband, my friend, with whom I collaborate to create a life of love, thank you.

As always, I am grateful to my editor, Mary Ann Hall, for her patience and guidance, to Betsy Gammons, my project manager, for her excellent shepherding of my book through the publication process. Thank you to Winnie Prentiss for the opportunity to share this book with you. And, thank you to David, Laura, Cora, and the other folks at Quarry Books who turn my collection of thoughts and ideas into a beautiful, finished book.